Uncoupling

Uncoupling

The Art of Coming Apart

NORMAN SHERESKY

and MARYA MANNES

NEW YORK THE VIKING PRESS

To husbands and wives everywhere,
and to Grace Marie

Preface

Over a hundred years ago President Lincoln, speaking about the myths that held many of us in bondage and turned many more into hostile adversaries, said, "We must disenthrall ourselves."

Now, after eleven decades, we are disenthralling ourselves with a vengeance from the myths of war, of race, of sex, and of social forms which we have accepted for many centuries as not only necessary but inevitable.

Of these, marriage has been the most durable thrall: the form in which most men and women and the State prefer to have their families reared, the condition that implies a joyous union of loving mates, a snug harbor in shifting human tides.

And, indeed, marriage serves some well. That it serves most not so well and many disastrously is a fact to which the zooming divorce rate year after year is only one evidence. Divorce is the dot on the "i" of a disintegration born of pain and anguish suffered by a man and a woman who expected too much, knew each other too little, and sought it as the only solution. That the pain inflicted by the solution itself is often as bad as, or worse than, the condition preceding it has only one cause: ignorance.

Just as we have turned our backs on dying, we have consistently ignored the psychological and sociological effects produced by the death of a marriage and the processes leading to its interment. Lawyer, psychiatrist, and psychologist are merely witnesses at the wake, too late to heal the wounds of the combatants. Much too late to have prevented needless suffering.

Because of this we feel that men and women themselves must look upon marriage with new eyes, must examine themselves and each other with new insights, and must, above all, learn what lies ahead of them when they turn to the law after all efforts to continue their union have foundered on bitterness, frustration, disillusionment, or hate.

And long before that, before they start blaming themselves or marriage itself for whatever disappointments and inadequacies begin to ravel the fabric of their union, they might find comfort in the fact that external forces beyond their control, and certainly not of their making, are stacked heavily against the institution of marriage itself.

One is time. Marriage as a form of living was never intended, historically, to bind two people for the length of time it now does, nor in the surroundings in which people now live. When the average life span was between twenty and thirty years, and when married couples and their families lived and worked in small self-sufficient agrarian units, the strains put upon wedlock were obviously far less than those placed upon the modern marriage. Among these strains, first and foremost, is the immense widening of human options due to communication. Before the automobile gave mobility to the citizens of even very small rural communities, they remained isolated from each other, confined not only by marriage but by the social strictures hemming them in. The man might drive his horse and buggy to the next town and find alternate pleasures, but the woman had no such choice.

Now, with urbanization and larger and larger communities, the chances of meeting other men and women, the kindling of new desires, grow much more frequent, presenting further alternatives to a frustrating or boring marriage. Add to this television and movies and the radical removal of restraints on sexual behavior in society as a whole in the wake of the sub-or-counter-culture, and men and women are made continually aware of sexual partnerships beyond and outside of marriage, and also of participation in group sex between married couples as well as single men and women. With all these options at hand, the survival of even a "good" marriage is easily threatened.

Good or bad, past or present, an institution centuries old and still accepted as a social necessity, marriage must rank as one of the least understood of all time.

For one thing, the selection of a mate is not rational, but emotional. Once a marriage has been contracted, however, the rational process not only can, but must, take over. The union can be intelligently observed by the two people involved and the pain produced by unsuccessful mating diminished or cut short with far less devastating effects than those too often suffered by married couples.

Because marriage is the repository of all forms of human emotion, it's easy to understand why its disintegration causes so much stress and personal anguish. Because it so often begins with undistilled and uncritical love—with total mutual acceptance—and so often ends in the total negation of one partner by the other through profound and open hatred, the effects on the participants at each stage between these extremes is powerful and sometimes immeasurable.

Yet the process of divorce, if it were understood, has limitations which are extremely beneficial, although largely unknown to most people. They would breathe much easier, for instance, if they knew that the ultimate that a judge can do—and the *only* things he can do—is dissolve a marriage, divide property, and award custody of children.

He cannot right wrongs, he cannot avenge one party against the other, he cannot rectify unfaithfulness, legislate "goodness," or repair bad marriages.

Divorce proceedings can and should be a rational process, as swift as possible, as painless as possible. This process should be as indifferent as possible to past mistakes, and to further rehashing or analysis of what wrongs were committed and by whom.

Society as a whole simply does not give a hoot why our marriages fail, and the propensity of divorcing couples for placing blame upon each other is idle, unconstructive, incredibly costly, and almost wholly irrelevant. Any satisfaction gained by either party is merely the residual sickness of rage.

The mass media and to a great extent the adversary system of justice—victor and vanquished, wrongdoer and victim—have created a monster. Divorce proceedings in television serials and faked-up, documentary-style divorce wrangles before judges would have us believe that divorce courts are places where the walking marital wounded are bandaged and soothed, and where swift retribution is meted out for marital wrongs. The kind of nonsense shown on the screen includes the sobbing wife (children and witnesses in tow), glaring at the unrepentant husband; the tough-talking F.-Lee-Bailey-type lawyer vying to show the patient actor-judge just how this party or that party fouled up the marriage, abused the other, irrevocably damaged the children's tender psyches, and otherwise shocked the community.

This is pure fabrication. Whenever a case gets as far as the trial stage in court, the first thing a judge tries to find out is who has been unreasonable—the clients or the lawyers—and why no settlement has been reached. With the lawyers in chambers and the clients waiting anxiously outside, the judge asks "How much?" and why shouldn't the mother get the children? Nothing more surely provokes judicial yawns than lawyers' attempts to tell the judge about tawdry love affairs and flagrant misdemeanors, true or false. Unless the story is a real pip, the judge has heard it before and will do anything to protect himself from having to hear it again.

And because these divorce proceedings are handled by two lawyers, each of whom is being paid to demonstrate his own abilities, what is fair is too often completely overlooked in favor of what can be gotten away with. Too many lawyers representing husbands feel they can justify their fees only by working out arrangements by which the husband pays too little. Too many wives' lawyers feel satisfied only when they can point out how little the husband is left with.

So long as we continue to regard divorce as an arena in which one party bests the other, and as a process by which emotional wounds can be healed, unnecessary pain and anguish and the expenditure of unnecessary legal fees and costs will be the inevitable results.

Once divorce is decided upon, and once the parties disclose truthfully and accurately their financial positions, fair and equitable divorce can and should result far more swiftly than most people imagine.

No book will ever instruct people on how to make better marriages, or on how to make unworkable marriages work, although the process by which marriages disintegrate can be far better understood. Many unhappy marriages are not so hopelessly shot that with better understanding they cannot be made more workable, and perhaps more enjoyable.

"Understanding" and "timing" are the key words here, for the longer honest confrontations are postponed by unhappy husbands and wives, the more steadily the chances for accommodation erode. The relationship founders in frustration, resignation, or boredom; communication ceases until the surgery of divorce becomes the only alternative to a state of war or an unendurable truce.

Yet surely the process of divorce itself can and should be better understood. In every real sense, divorce is the beginning of new lives for the husband, the wife, and the children: lives that should not be launched against a background of acrimony and anguish. Husbands should not face their future burdened by agreements or court orders that they cannot hope to comply with, nor by continuous servitude to families they no longer have. Wives should not be expected to make new lives under agreements or court orders which consign them to a life of penury and confinement with their children. The myth that all women, regardless of how inept or how crippled they may have become as a result of the marital relationship, are on a parity with men and should go out and get work and support themselves is a cruel theoretical hoax. For those women, married a short time and undamaged by the rigors of an unhappy union, there need be considerably less concern.

This is especially true of the woman who has a job giving her at least some degree of economic independence, or a profession endowing her not only with a sense of identity as an individual human being but with an outlet for resources of mind and spirit.

What is fair for the family unit in the future must guide the courts and lawyers. What will pay back the partners for the wrongs they have each committed must be ignored.

While much of this book will deal with how to achieve this goal of a fair and equitable settlement as painlessly as possible, we do not lose sight of the general need for guidance in the system as it exists today. Where reason and knowledge are in short supply, intelligent alternatives are available to the client and the lawyer, many of which are examined, along with their consequences. Even a reasonable client and a knowledgeable lawyer can hardly sit back and be bludgeoned into accepting disastrous agreements by the highhandedness, shenanigans, and matrimonial ploys of those intent more on victory than on equity. We thus examine a sampling of the strategies of matrimonial warfare. It will be seen how pathetically unnecessary they are and how they simply prolong the battle without improving the result.

Much of the fear about divorce is justified. It can be painful, irrevocably destructive, and, as a cure, worse than the disease. However, the parties to divorce and their counselors are too often the cause of all this pain. It is simply asinine to submit the fate of mature people and their children to judicial roulette. To ask a judge in a matter of hours, or even days, to impose conditions upon families that they have to live with for the rest of their lives is to take a risk which should be avoided at all costs.

It is far better to get rid of the lawyers who cannot agree over a period of months on what is fair than to expose the clients to the uncertainties and vagaries of the judicial process. Where the lawyers cannot agree because the clients are unreasonable, it is very often preferable for the lawyers to get rid of the clients than to expose them to the risks they sometimes needlessly take.

Our divorce laws are getting better and better. For example, in matters concerning the custody and welfare of children, they are quite acceptable and workable when they are not punitive. However, the entire adversary process makes the courtroom a poor setting for complex problems of divorce. Judges are harried and unpredictable: their decisions reflect their own backgrounds and their own experiences in marriage. Judges in different courts and different judges in the same court very often render entirely disparate decisions on almost identical sets of facts. In matters matrimonial, courts should surely be the place of last resort.

Contents

Uncoupling

CHAPTER 1

How Bad Is Your Marriage?

A couple in their early forties are having dinner in a restaurant. They eat, but they do not talk. They look, but not at each other. Their eyes and ears are turned toward a pair on the banquette opposite: a man and a woman locked in each other's gaze, speaking softly, inaudibly, sometimes laughing together, holding each other's hand on the table.

The older, speechless couple shrivels inside. Were they ever like that? And if they were, what happened? They are, of course, the sepulcher of a dead marriage; a man and woman who once thought they had it made and failed or refused to recognize the signals indicating—flash by flash, over two decades —that they hadn't.

Like nations locked in hopeless wars, they refuse to admit failure. It would be easy to break this down into failure in sex and failure in communication, but this is the end, not the beginning. Too late for sex manuals, too late for psychiatry, too late for empathy: the single greatest quality of love. Having failed to feel for each other, feeling has turned either into the mute hatred of the trapped or the desperate boredom of the habitual.

What are the signals they missed along the way? Some very obvious ones would include a mutual inability to agree on primary matters, like money, savings, and division of property.

Like having children and raising them.

3

Like the acceptance or rejection of each other's friends and relatives.

Like sexual dissatisfaction: the slow ebbing of mutual desire, or—even worse—a greater tension of need in one partner than in the other. To turn toward a body that does not turn to yours can become intolerable, leading inevitably to a search for satisfactions outside the home for one and mute frustration for the other.

These signals of incompatibility are common to both men and women, but there are real differences between the sexes in the matter of awareness. Women are far more prone to face and to name the realities than men, and more anxious to rectify them. And here we come to communication: an art, a weapon, and an indulgence which women use far more adroitly in the realm of intimate human relations than men.

Men save their words for their professions, for the intra-personal relations of their business; in their homes, they are no match for articulate wives.

Talk is their enemy, pounding at the gates of their virility, threatening their self-assumptions; and from too many wives it has become a continual static of triviality that drains their men of desire or interest. The word "communication" can also take on an ominous meaning for married couples. Where it should imply the ability to exchange views without intimidation, it has come to mean a license to many women to talk their husbands into a state of exhaustion. The insufferable "girl-talk" of the TV-commercial housewives may be a traversty of women as a whole, but there is every reason why the returned commuter-husband should dive for a drink or a tranquilizer when his wife starts telling him about the leaking faucet the minute he gets in the door. Saying the wrong thing at the wrong time, for that matter, is the greatest diminisher of sex-appetite since saltpeter. In this battle of communication, the silent husband—exasperating as he might seem—comes off best. In communicating for peace, he comes off worst.

Professor Higgins wants to know "Why can't a woman—be

more like a man?" One reason is that she lacks a man's capacity for burying his head in the sand when it comes to his marriage. Her ability to face marital problems head-on and the pain of marital introspection in general far exceeds that of her husband.

It is not that she, presumably unlike him, is unconcerned by world events, or less distracted by sports and gadgetry, but rather that she has a strong sense of priorities and puts her family and her relationship to it in a predominant position. Few marriage counselors and psychiatrists would disagree that the wife is the first to know and the first to try to do something about marital discord.

Yet while few men realize the legitimate need of women to talk and to be taken seriously, few women in turn realize the range of demands made upon a husband. A husband faced with severe business problems or financial difficulty does not get the same sense of release through "communication" as does a woman. Professional or financial failure is a threat to a man's virility, and when a man feels vulnerable, he senses communication as a desire on the part of his woman to out-talk him and to out-smart him. Because women are far often more articulate, fluent, and knowledgeable about matters relating to their marriages, they should realize that their husbands shy from verbal scrimmages in which they don't excel, particularly when they are in a weakened condition.

Men also tend to resist verbalizing about sex: an inability which can, and very often does, work against mutual sexual release. While most marital disagreements involve verbal eruptions, those concerning sex are the most sinister because they are silent, repressive, guilt-laden, and misunderstood.

The paradox here is that total honesty can be more dangerous than partial deception. And again, only empathy—the ability to put oneself in another's skin—can maintain this delicate balance between reality and illusion.

The disintegration of a marriage is almost universally ignored until it is too late because it spells failure to the participants and to the spectators: society.

To a matrimonial lawyer, there seems virtually no case in which both parties seeking or acquiescing in a divorce did not consider themselves to be failures. This is doubly curious because, while many marriages fail, there is actually little correlation between the fact of failure and the fact of the success or failure of either participant. Very often one or both parties outgrow the relationship, and the neurotic marriage is simply unsuited to the growth and success of either or both of the participants.

Another myth of marital failure is the curious notion that a description of the marriage also describes its participants. It is simply not true that a good or "happy" marriage consists of the union between two good or two happy people, or that a bad or unhappy marriage consists of unstable or unloving partners. A combination of ruthless or weak people may produce extremely workable marriages, and disaster may dog the union of extremely well-adjusted and/or productive people.

For whatever reason, by the time people consult their lawyers today, their marriage is pretty well shot. This was not always so when there were more legal general practitioners, fewer psychiatrists, marriage counselors, and psychologists, and less talk about the relief and freedom of divorce.

Today the lawyer is usually the last to know. He hears "I can't stand it any more," "She's left," "I want to take the son-of-a-bitch for everything he has," a lot more than he hears "Can I make a go of it?" "What is wrong?" "Can it be corrected?"

But there are "bad marriages" that don't deserve to be junked, that with some effort can be made workable; and in few cases a trained lawyer will apply his skills toward dissuading his client from too precipitous action. So, how can you tell whether your marriage is as lousy as you think it is or suspect it might be?

You can tell you've gone as far with self-diagnosis as you can when you're tired of asking yourself the same questions, and when your friends are tired of hearing the same complaints. Then you seek help. From whom? From somebody who can be objective and whose experience ranges wider than your thrice-divorced Auntie Mame or your friend Sid who has been having a "ball" since he unloaded that shrew who made him so unhappy. You wouldn't let your pre-med nephew who has done one hundred twenty-five frog dissections take out your gall bladder, so why would you let less experienced relatives and friends tamper with your marriage?

For an operation severing the connective tissues—physical, spiritual, emotional—between a man and woman the rational would choose an expert. This should mean a lawyer, although we'll explore alternatives later. Regardless of whom you choose, however, be sure that the person consulted is on the same wave length as you are. An elderly lawyer who is on the faculty of Fordham, say, and a trustee of several churches is a poor judge of the vitality of a marriage between teen-age jet-setters who haven't settled down yet. And a swinging mod lawyer is hardly in a position to advise an elderly couple plagued by a severe combination of geriatric and legal problems.

Marriage can be defined, for example, as an institution which is necessary, convenient, ever-changing, stultifying, constricting, boredom-laden, or simply bad for a lot of people. *My* opinion of *your* marriage may be objective in terms of *you*, but it is so only in the light of my own feelings about marriage. If you think that a marriage without controversy is desirable, or that a marriage even without love is possible, then *my* views of how bad your marriage is are irrelevant.

Yet your marriage *is* bad when you feel that you can function better without your spouse than with him. It is bad when you would rather be alone or with somebody else than with him; not sometimes, but usually. It is bad when you think that your children would profit from the absence of a particular parent.

A marriage is getting bad if there is appreciably less fun. It is truly bad when there is no more fun at all.

Bad marriages can also be described in terms of the nature of the mates and the sort of behavior permitted, fostered, and nurtured by them. Yet although these factors may *theoretically* indicate a bad marriage, the couple may be quite successful (if rarely "happy") in their behavior patterns, and quite unwilling to exchange them for others.

Compulsive gamblers and alcoholics married to "rescuers," sexually deviant couples (such as transvestites or sadomasochists), and compulsive spenders are among those who often prefer their weird worlds to more "acceptable" alternatives. There are many marital cripples who, deprived of strong medical support, should be left with what little they have rather than encouraged to break their shells and expose themselves singly to a hostile society and their own vulnerability.

When, then, should a bad marriage end in divorce? Whenever it is clear that its destructiveness is irreversible, or only reversible with effort which is clearly not forthcoming from either partner.

Furthermore, it must be determined that divorce, as an alternative for a particular couple, has a real chance. Most people contemplating such a serious step should consider what they will do when the ties are severed.

Yet they rarely do. The age, intelligence, financial prospects, number of children, and cultural background of divorce prospects (even the city and state where both or either may live, urban or suburban) are vital factors to be weighed before the definitive plunge. More serious, in fact, than the attitudes of family or friends, or of people like you or us.

Yet these factors are widely ignored. In the two crucial human decisions—to marry and to divorce—knowledge and reason play the smallest part. Most people do not want to face what faces them.

CHAPTER 2

Marriage: A Little Knowledge Goes a Short Way

Americans are dreamers. We marry out of hope, and we hope that our dreams will come true.

That is why we continue to marry even though the United States has the largest divorce rate in the world. We are a mobile and unauthoritarian people, increasingly rootless, shedding our past, evading our future. We live for today and shut out the reality of tomorrow in the same way that we shut out the reality of death.

People marry when there is a curious and too often temporary alignment of expectations and need between a man and a woman. We are attracted to our partners because they promise a fulfillment of ourselves, because they satisfy our sexual appetites, because they seem to enlarge our sense of living and loving—now.

Our vision is temporary. It is also still strongly affected by social attitudes concerned (as they have been for centuries) less with enduring love than with appearances. Ingrained in a majority of women is the belief that marriage combines the ideal poles of escape and security: escape from parents or the burden of single identity in the form of work or career; security in the arms and home of the protector-provider.

Nor is the man immune from the nudgings of social convenience and convention. A wife is good for business. A wife can supply comforts few bachelors care to be bothered with. And sex? No lack of it anywhere, but he dreams of the sweetness of not having to leave the beds of others at dawn; of feasting at will.

These and the dream of love cloud deeper insights. We refuse to believe that wives can tire of mothering husbands, and husbands can tire of being surrogate fathers. Sooner or later the roles demanded by married people of each other change, and the woman who served as a splendid substitute-Mom may founder dismally as a wife. So may the bridegroom-stud fail, in due course, as the father-adviser his young bride really craved.

We marry for the damndest reasons. A man may want a hostess, an accessory, a centerfold, a sister, a slave, or a tyrant. A woman may crave a tycoon, a stud, a brother, a brute, or a son.

Besides seeking mates who seemingly are able to satisfy our *present* sexual needs and our *present* needs for familial substitution, we also have other individual present needs for which we more or less unconsciously seek satisfaction. If we are drug addicts, alcoholics, or people with other compulsive habits, we tend to find mates who will satisfy us by punishing us for our habits or by continually trying to rescue us from them. If we are insecure self-doubters, we may seek the satisfaction of marrying mates whose frailties loom even larger, and whom we may criticize. If we are inefficient and unproductive, we may seek even worse bunglers from whose failures we derive consolation. If we are lonely and afraid, we may seek anybody who will give us the temporary relief of filling time and space. Very often we marry for the same reason that others take pills—"uppers" or "downers"—simply to change our state of being.

We seldom ask whether he or she will make a good lover, a good parent, or a good companion ten years from now. And very few of us, in a civilization where intellect is a minor desideratum (especially in a woman), suspect that its absence may lead in time to excruciating boredom.

Marriages crumble, finally, when each blames the other for failing to embody the original visions that impelled their union:

"I would have made something of myself if it weren't for you!" or, "I could have married anybody I wanted. Why did I have to choose you?"

Why, indeed? But even if we chose wisely in the light of an apparent alignment of mutual needs, the crack in the marriage foundation that splits wide open is, simply, ignorance—an appalling ignorance of the realistic obligations of marriage itself.

Of these, ironically, ignorance about the true nature of love is a major marital fission. Ironically, because we now appear to know everything we ever wanted to know about sex, and are bombarded daily with manuals on how to please everybody forever. Americans spend millions of dollars annually making the producers of smut and pornography wealthy because we can now allow ourselves to be openly titillated and triumphantly prurient.

It is still too early to know whether all this open sex, openly arrived at, will improve marriage or ultimately destroy its vital intimacies.

What we do know, beyond a doubt, is that ignorance about sex has been responsible for the wreck of an enormous number of marriages. We are the victims of a Puritan heritage, equating sex with sin, that has left Americans with a host of inhibitions crippling to the spirit as well as the senses, turning beauty into shame, and joy into guilt. This process, in the name of Morality, has been, in fact, a denial of humanity.

In redressing the balance, the pendulum may have swung too far in making sex not only a commodity but a substitute for love, a public performance rather than a private experience.

Yet serious students of sex, like Masters and Johnson, have made important and useful contributions to the knowledge of our sexual selves which have already saved some foundering marriages and could, if translated into less abstruse language, rescue many more.

There exists, in any case, a whole body of information about the sexual problems of marriage that is now ready to be imparted to us if it were made available in simple terms. That it isn't may well reflect society's belief that we are not to be trusted with it. Instead—and again ironically—we are deluged with nonbooks by nonwriters (*The Sensuous Woman, The Sensuous Man*), which cater to an intelligent audience as well as pizzas appease fastidious palates.

This escalation of expectation is not only a major reason why marriages fail, but why they take place. Both partners persist in believing that the sexual pleasures they enjoy before or anticipate when they marry, will last forever, without further knowledge, effort, or growth on their part.

And what of our overwhelming ignorance about the obligations we took on by law when we marry? Any law student will tell you that a contract cannot exist unless the parties to it agree to each of its essential terms. But we all know that when we said, in a state of trembling euphoria, "I do," we weren't agreeing to any of these terms because—quite simply—no such contract ever existed.

If you are of sufficient age and mental capacity; if you are free of some diseases (but not all); if you are not a prisoner and not already married, you are free—according to the state—to marry anybody possessing the same negative assets, provided, however, that they are of the opposite sex.

If John, hating babies, doting on rock, disdaining all Republicans, and believing whole-heartedly in the overthrow of the United States Government by any means whatever, can convince Joan for a continuous period rarely in excess of seventy-two hours, to marry him, the state has no objection whatsoever to such portentous facts as that Joan loves large families, likes classical music, is a member of the Republican National Committee, is proud of the United States Marine Corps, and believes in the sanctity of J. Edgar Hoover.

The state will let you in the marriage game for the price of a license, and out at the price of a heart transplant.

Why does the state interfere in our lives anyway?

Why does it permit us to live alone virtually without restriction, but in New York, for example, harness us once we are married, with several hundreds of sections of the Domestic Relations Law, the Family Court Act and Rules, and other related statutes and decisions?

It seems that our legislators feel that marriages are not to be lightly discarded, even if they have been lightly contracted.

One of the reasons, then, why marriages so frequently fail is that they are usually entered into at a time of our lives when we are least able to exercise sound judgment about our priorities.

Inflamed by passion, consumed by hope, giddy with love, we enter into matrimonial transactions without even the questionable objectivity we display in choosing a new car. Objectivity and love are very seldom partners at any time, in any case.

Consider, for instance, what would happen to the institution of marriage if the parties were required to familiarize themselves with the rules of the game. (After all, we do take drivers' tests.)

What if we required all married couples to show some basic familiarity with the laws that govern their relationship, and some familiarity with each other's views on the essential ingredients of the relationship?

For example, whether to have children and when, who should own what property, who is obligated to work; financial penalties, if any, if the wife doesn't work and takes care of the children; consequences of the insanity or incapacity of the other spouse; the consequences of inviting widower-Dad to join the household indefinitely. Or, for example, the consequences of Change of Heart? Why does the state license a thoughtless marriage for life, but condemn one between two people who genuinely love and care for each other, who have honestly considered the essential terms of their contemplated agreement, but who want to commit themselves only for a period of two or three years?

Because the state is atrophied in patterns of the past inapplicable to present realities. So, if you are married, it is already too late.

But it is not too late for us to change our own minds about

the process of choosing our mates. It is possible, if not enjoyable, to put a damper on our enthusiasm just long enough to inquire seriously about the contemplated relationship, about why we are marrying in the first place.

We are obliged, by law, to divulge to each other some of the most essential facts about ourselves so that we cannot, after the state has joined us, be charged with fraud. Concealing prior marriages, hereditary diseases, past imprisonments, unwillingness to become parents, affiliations with dubious organizations, may result in annulments and divorces based on fraud.

Having told the truth to each other, there are other obligations. The parties must at least occasionally engage in sexual relations. There is, of course, not the slightest obligation to enjoy such activities and not a single regulation involving frequency.

There is no statutory obligation to love, honor, or obey, except that wives may not refuse to cohabit with husbands in such reasonable places as the husband may designate. Each partner in a marriage must insulate the state, however, against the cost of supporting the other and the children of the marriage. The state, for instance, will not pay for the hospitalization of the husband if the wife can afford to foot the bill.

There are a host of other obligations that arise out of the marital relation, and which involve the ownership of property. Husbands and wives may now own property separate and apart from each other. They may contract with each other and sue each other. But since contracts between husbands and wives are scrutinized by courts and since each is assumed to have a duty to treat the other fairly and openly, contractual rights may be obliterated and "implied obligations" may be created where the husband or wife has acted unfairly to the other.

It is an extremely common occurrence for husbands and wives faced with impending divorce to claim that all of the property, real or personal, standing in the name of one spouse was always really intended by both parties to be joint property. There are a myriad of conflicting statutes and decisions that question the status of real or personal property, whether or not it is held individually or jointly. In matters matrimonial it is not that the decisions or the statues are unclear, but rather that judges hesitate to apply them with the rigidity accorded to routine commercial transactions. It is one thing to say that Joan is entitled to maintain her own bank account, but quite another when it turns out that Joan has been depositing John's checks and other funds which John didn't know about (such as the food budget) into her own account. It is perfectly all right for John to put the house in his name, but when the judge finds out that he got all the money from Joan and her parents and told her that he was only putting the house in his name to increase his borrowing capacity for business, and when it turns out his borrowing capacity has been used to augment his passion for the ponies, the judge takes a different view.

But now we come—in the light of our revolutionary times and the progressive blurring of sex "roles"—to the real clincher. The state maintains that a husband has a duty of which he may not relieve himself—that of supporting his wife and children. A few states make this obligation of support mutual and in an appropriate case may require a wife to support a husband.

But what are the rules concerning alimony? They are incomprehensible, that's what they are. Although the laws vary widely from state to state, any knowledgeable attorney knows they also vary widely and inconsistently even within any single state. In some states alimony is considered to be, in part, a punishment or a reward.

Rarely, however, is it the husband who is punished for his misconduct in terms of alimony. When he has to pay it, it doesn't matter (theoretically, at least) whether he has sinned a little or a lot or not at all.

To a wife, the difference may be vital. In most states, fault plays a crucial aspect in how much support a wife may receive for herself. In New York, for example, under the "liberalized" reform law, a court may not award support to a wife where she is guilty of such misconduct as would entitle her husband to a decree of divorce. If, for example, a wife learned that her husband had been having an affair for seventeen years with her sister, and that the children had been denied a college education because her husband also had another mistress, set up in a Park Avenue penthouse, she would not be entitled to support if it is learned that during an evening of anguish and indiscretion caused by such disclosures she was intimate with her psychiatrist. Even in California, which has a genuine no-fault divorce law, attorneys for husbands still attempt to let the judge know when the wife is at fault. For example, although the word "adultery" is theoretically meaningless and has no statutory significance, the husband's lawyer is bound to ask the wife, "Why do you need so much money for food? Isn't Mr. X staying with you and paying these bills?"

Like other states, New York by statute requires the courts, when fixing alimony, to take into consideration the ability of the wife to work. Yet some decisions frequently reflect the court's reluctance to punish working wives by diminishing their assets and preventing them from saving from inadequate salaries, particularly where the husband's assets and income are substantial compared to the wife's.

We have rules, decisions, and statutes instructing the judge that wives should not be permitted to become "alimony drones"; that they should not be permitted to become self-indulgent, indolent parasites. These compete with other rules, statutes, and decisions directing that the court take into consideration the length of the marriage, the age of the wife, the age of the children, and a preseparation standard of living.

What all this means is that in matters matrimonial the issue of alimony is no more certain than a roll of the dice in Las Vegas, and the consequences to the litigants may be just as disastrous as they are to the gamblers, yet how often do engaged couples consider this crucial subject in advance? Or their feelings about child support? Or whether their assets and joint income should be divided or undivided? Why should a woman whose husband has permitted her and encouraged her to become a marital cripple with no economic potential be treated on a parity with a woman whose earning capacity has not been influenced or deterred by the marriage at all?

More importantly, why shouldn't the parties themselves make the rules before there is trouble? Why shouldn't the standard of support be agreed upon before it is imposed upon the parties? Why is it not just as sensible for newlyweds to agree on what standard or standards they wish imposed rather than to rely upon a judge to whom marriage may have an entirely different meaning?

Why do lawyers arrogate to themselves the function of dissuading women who truly do not want or do not feel entitled to alimony? Why do lawyers attempt to persuade their male clients to give less than they might wish to give voluntarily?

Decades of litigation, under a variety of different statutes and decisions, have shown that it is far better for people to agree to the rules themselves than to rely upon the courts to intervene. Obviously agreements would be reached far sooner if the parties to a marriage knew what the rules were as they went along. It occurs to us that a great many people might never get married at all if they were required beforehand to examine in depth their real reasons for taking this step.

What would happen if an engaged couple, Donald Brown and Ina Jones, decided to consider in advance of their marriage issues and questions which might emerge later concerning their physical, financial, and emotional attitudes and preferences? What if they wanted a document that would provide a solid basis from which to resolve future disputes? What if they wanted to have available to them a historical reminder of how they once felt? Less poetically, what if they agreed to come clean in a calm and loving atmosphere that would probably not exist if they came to the end of their marital tether?

We set forth here such an agreement between such a couple,

one which is no doubt invalid in every state, but which highlights the kinds of questions which "newlyweds" rarely come to grips with during the engagement period:

MEMORANDUM OF UNDERSTANDING AND INTENT made this ——day of July, 1972, between DONALD BROWN, residing at —— City, County, and State of New York, herein called DONALD, and INA JONES, residing at —— City, County, and State of New York, herein called INA.

WHEREAS the parties are about to marry and in anticipation of that event they desire to make full and fair disclosure to each other of those facts and circumstances concerning their lives which they deem essential and significant; and

WHEREAS the parties desire to make full and fair disclosure of their attitudes and expectations concerning their future and the future of any children born to them from the pending marriage; and

WHEREAS the parties desire to fix and determine by this ante-nuptial agreement the rights and claims that will accrue to each of them in the estate and property of the other by reason of the marriage.

IT IS MUTUALLY AGREED AS FOLLOWS:

ARTICLE I
Declaration of Marital Intention

(a) DONALD and INA each declares to the other the unequivocal intention to marry in the City, County, and State of New York on or before September——, 1972.

(b) This marriage is freely and voluntarily being entered into out of mutual love and respect held by the parties for each other, and neither party has agreed to enter this marriage under any threats, emotional or otherwise, nor has any relative or either of the parties exercised any undue influence upon either DONALD or INA.

(c) Each party assures the other that he or she has had sufficient time and sufficient information to make the decision to marry in accordance with the terms and provisions of this Memorandum.

ARTICLE II
Historical Representation

A. DONALD hereby represents and warrants to INA and expects her to act in reliance upon such representations and warranties:

(a) He is twenty-nine years old; he attended the University of —— from which he graduated in — with a bachelor of —— degree and with acceptable but unexceptional grades.

(b) His mother and father are living and until February 1963 he continued to reside with them and contributed toward their support, and he still occasionally contributes toward their support and intends to continue to the extent that he is able during marriage. DONALD's parents react favorably to the contemplated marriage. They are unable to make any financial contributions to the marriage. DONALD's parents have not been divorced. His older brother has been divorced twice and his sister is contemplating divorce.

(c) DONALD was previously married in April 1963 and that marriage ended in a divorce in June 1970. There is one child of that marriage, MICHAEL, age six. The decree of divorce was handed down by the Supreme Court, New York County, and awarded custody of MICHAEL to DONALD's former wife, granted alimony and child support in the sum of $140.00 weekly, and further granted DONALD visitation privileges every other weekend and for longer periods during holidays and summertime. A copy of the divorce decree has been shown to INA, has been read by her, and is annexed hereto and marked Exhibit A.

(d) There is no history of mental illness in DONALD's family presently known to DONALD, except that one of his brothers has from time to time consulted with a psychiatrist for what are believed to be personal emotional problems. There are no hereditary or other diseases prevalent in DONALD's family and DONALD is in excellent physical health.

(e) There is no history of any arrest or conviction of DONALD for any criminal behavior, nor is there any history of any habitual compulsive addiction such as to drugs, alcohol, gambling, etc.

(f) DONALD is presently employed as an assistant sales manager for ABC Company at a salary of $22,500.00 annually, including bonuses, and exclusive of certain travel and entertainment expenses which are made available to him by his employer. His salary during the three previous years was as follows:

$$1969—\$14,500.00$$
$$1970—\$17,500.00$$
$$1971—\$18,500.00$$

Further financial information relating to DONALD is hereinafter set forth in Article V.

(g) The relationship between DONALD with his parents and with his brothers and sister have been explained fully to INA.

DONALD and INA have discussed at length the "tradition" of a two-week family sojourn made every year to the Brown residence in Pennsylvania and DONALD's desire to continue that tradition. INA has expressed a reluctance to adhere to that tradition, but agrees to be bound by DONALD's wishes. With respect to other familial visitations, DONALD has agreed that he will make no arrangements for such visitations without the consent of INA and he agrees that such visitation (either at his and INA's home or at the home of the Jones family) should be no more frequent than twice monthly.

(h) DONALD had disclosed to INA that his relationship with his past wife was and continues to be strained. He has disclosed to her that on at least two prior occasions he and his former wife have been involved in legal proceedings relating to the custody and amount of support of MICHAEL. The nature of such proceedings, the reasons therefore, and all other questions of INA's concerning them have been fully explored by the parties.

DONALD's relationship with MICHAEL has been fully explored by the parties. It is DONALD's present feeling that the time may arise in the future when he would wish to gain custody of MICHAEL, and INA's reluctance for a period of at least two years to have such custody have been considered by the

exist, INA shall either have demonstrated or expressed, and such issues as frequency of intercourse, desire for periods of abstention, positions of intercourse, etc., have been explored to INA's satisfaction.

(f) INA is presently employed as an assistant interior decorator for the BCD Department Store and her salary this past year was $6300.00.

(g) There is no history of compulsive addiction such as to drugs, alcohol, gambling, etc.

ARTICLE III
Future Expectations

(a) DONALD and INA have discussed fully their intentions concerning where they propose to reside during the course of their marriage. They agree jointly that considerations relating to the location of their respective families should play no part in such determination. They agree the primary consideration shall be that their place of residence be in close proximity to DONALD's place of business. That factor should govern regardless of where INA may be employed, and regardless of the disparity, if any, between their respective salaries.

(b) Neither party to this Memorandum holds any formal religious beliefs which should in any way interfere with the marriage. Neither insists on, or even has expressed any preference concerning, the other's adherence to any particular religious belief, and neither will insist, without the consent of the other, upon imposing any religious belief upon any children of the marriage.

(c) It is the parties' present intention that INA continue to work and that, her health permitting, she continue to do so until such time as she may become pregnant. The parties have no exact intentions concerning the employment of INA after the birth of any child or children, although she has expressed her present feelings as being that she would not find caring for children to be sufficiently stimulating to her. DONALD's inclination at the present time is that he would prefer INA to discontinue any full-time employment, but that he would not insist upon it.

Both parties agree that any subsequent employment of INA after the birth of any child should not be such that it would not permit her to spend reasonable periods of time with the child and should not entail any evening or weekend hours.

(d) Both DONALD and INA have each expressed reasonably strong condemnation of adultery and DONALD has expressed the view that he would immediately divorce INA if such act on her part occurred, regardless of the circumstances. INA has said that although she does not wish to solicit such conduct on the part of DONALD, nevertheless, she is unable to express what her attitude would be if DONALD committed adultery without knowing what the circumstances were. If it were an isolated "meaningless" episode, INA's opinion is that she would rather not know of it because she does not know how it would affect her relationship with DONALD.

Both parties have agreed that in the event that either engages in any serious or prolonged affair with anyone else, he or she is under an obligation to disclose that fact to the other.

Each party believes that his present sex life with the other is sufficiently pleasurable and knowledgeable so that no serious or material adjustment need be made by either. INA has expressed her belief that her sex life with DONALD will become more pleasurable and somewhat less tense after marriage, and after each party has had more "experience" with each other. She denied having, however, any apprehension concerning any future sexual relations with DONALD.

(e) The parties intend having children of their own, and expect to have two or three children. It is their desire to have such children sometime after the next two years, although the possibility of having a child prior to that time does not cause any particular anxiety in either of them. In the event that INA becomes pregnant mistakenly, the parties' present inclination is to have such child and not seek abortion. Both parties feel that any such decision should be left entirely to INA in her absolute and uncontrolled discretion.

(f) In addition to the foregoing subjects, DONALD and INA have discussed and have rejected the following notions: marriage of limited duration, separate vacations, separate beds, divorce by reason of the physical (but not mental) incapacity of the other, divorce by reason of the inability of INA to bear children.

(g) In the event that for any reason INA is unable to bear children, the parties are in conflict over whether to adopt a child. It would be INA's desire under such circumstances to adopt a child and it is DONALD's strong feeling that he would not. Although the parties agree that this eventually would be of considerable importance to them, they feel that it is better to leave that issue undetermined prior to such an eventuality arising.

ARTICLE IV
Future Support

(a) In the event that either party desires a separation (physical or legal) or divorce during the first five years of marriage (unless a child is born of the marriage and is alive at such time), neither party will request support from the other unless he or she is in dire need thereof, and for only such temporary period as may be determined to be necessary in accordance with Article VIII hereof.

(b) In the event that either party desires a separation (physical or legal) after the first five years of marriage or in the event that at such time a child of the marriage is alive, either party may request support which shall be granted or denied in accordance with Article VIII hereof. The arbitrator shall consider the length of the marriage, the number of children, their ages, the age of the parties, and their health; the ability of INA to work, the number of years that INA has been unemployed and the reasons therefor, and INA's realistic chances of being productively employed; the disparity between the parties income and income-earning potential; the amount of property to be divided between them in accordance with this agreement; which party desires such separation or divorce and the reasons therefor; Donald's legal obligations to his former wife and to his son, Michael; and the preseparation standard of living provided such standard was reasonable. No factor shall be conclusive and the award, if any, will be such as to do substantial justice between the parties considering all factors.

ARTICLE V
Division of Property

(a) DONALD presently has a checking account at the Manufacturers Hanover Trust Company, 46th Street and Lexington Avenue, the present balance of which is $1685.50. He has a savings account at the Greenwich Savings Bank (Branch No. —— Account No. ——), the balance of which is $3750.00.

(b) INA presently has a checking account in her own name at the National City Bank, Park Avenue and 52nd Street, the present balance of which is $385.00. She maintains a savings account at the same bank (Account No. ——), the present balance of which is $950.00.

(c) DONALD owns four hundred shares of XYZ Corporation, which is traded on the New York Stock Exchange and which has a present value of $4000 and he owns no other securities. DONALD is also the owner of a 1970 Buick Riviera, upon which there is presently due $650.00 in installment obligations.

(d) INA owns no securities and does not own an automobile.

(e) Neither party owns any real property.

ARTICLE VI
Future Ownership of Property

(a) DONALD and INA have agreed that until their marriage all property standing in the name of either shall be continued to be held in the individual names of the parties owning such property.

(b) Upon the marriage of DONALD and INA they will create a joint-checking and a joint-savings account to which each shall contribute in the same proportion as their joint salaries and bonuses bear to each other. In the event that the parties or either of them decide to seek a separation or divorce

within a period of thirty-six months from the date of their
marriage or at any time prior to the birth of a child, the proceeds of such checking account and savings account shall be
divided in the same proportion in which such funds were contributed by the parties. If either party seeks a separation or
divorce after the birth of a child or at the end of said thirty-
six-month-period, whichever is earlier, such proceeds shall be
divided between the parties equally.

(c) In the event that INA is unable to find employment or
during any periods of involuntary unemployment or during
any period of maternity or illness during which she is unable
to work, her contributions to the joint funds during the period
of such unemployment, illness, or maternity shall be deemed
to have been in direct proportion to the contributions previously made by her during the period immediately preceding such loss of employment, illness, or maternity.

(d) DONALD and INA will jointly receive and maintain in a
place in their home, accessible to both, all financial records of
and all bank accounts maintained by either of them, as well
as any and all records concerning the ownership of any personal or real property held by them individually or jointly.

(e) All questions concerning the investment of the joint
funds of DONALD and INA in securities or real estate shall be
decided jointly by the parties and the ownership and division
of such real or personal property should be made in accordance with paragraphs (a) and (c) hereof.

(f) The parties do not contemplate a different division of
property, real or personal, whether or not either or both may
be guilty of any misconduct as defined by the laws of the
State of New York. Any property held by either of the parties
not in accordance with the terms of this paragraph shall be
deemed to be held in trust for the other party and there have
been and there will be no private or oral understandings between the parties concerning the division of property between
them, unless in writing.

(g) All wedding gifts or gifts from parents, friends, or other
third parties during the course of the marriage shall be
deemed by the parties to be owned equally unless such gifts
or others which can only be used or enjoyed by the party to

whom such gift is made individually (e.g., ladies' wrist watch, man's golf clubs, etc.).

(h) In the event that either DONALD or INA subsequently wishes to change the rules by which their property shall be divided, the party desiring such change shall notify the other in writing and by registered mail at least one hundred and twenty days prior to such proposed change. If the other party does not wish to make such change, he or she may notify the other party of such decision within one hundred and twenty days and in writing, and the matter shall be resolved by arbitration in accordance with the terms of Article VIII hereof. In making its determination any arbitrator shall fully inquire into the facts and circumstances surrounding the reason or reasons for the proposed desired change and no modification of existing financial arrangements shall be made if it is determined that a substantial reason for such proposed change is the imminent expectation of either of the parties of coming into a sudden period of prosperity in which it is not desired by the party seeking modification to include the other party. The arbitrator may consider such other factors as he wishes in order to do substantial justice between the parties, but he may not order any modification of the rules by which the parties have agreed to divide the property retroactive to the period preceding the one-hundred-and-twenty-day-period succeeding the written request for modification.

ARTICLE VII
Matters of Estate

(a) For the first thirty-six months of the marriage between DONALD and INA neither party shall be required to leave any portion of his or her estate to the other except the minimal amount required by State law.

(b) After thirty-six months of marriage each party agrees to leave the other at least one third of his or her entire estate and each agrees to make no attempt to assign, transfer, or otherwise dispose of, without valuable consideration, any portion of his or her estate with the intention of depriving the other of the full benefits of this agreement.

ARTICLE VIII
Arbitration

Any dispute which arises under the terms of this Memorandum shall be resolved in accordance with the rules and regulations then obtaining of the American Arbitration Association, and such arbitration shall be held in the City, County, and State of New York, unless both parties reside in some other state in which event such arbitration shall take place in that state.

ARTICLE IX
Mutual Waiver

Each of the parties to this Memorandum recognizes that it may be partially or wholly illegal in the State of New York or in some subsequent state in which either or both parties may subsequently reside. To the extent that this agreement, or any part thereof, is unenforceable, the parties waive all privileges and agree that to the extent permitted by state law, such agreement may be used in any action for separation or divorce instituted by either party against the other as evidence of the parties' intentions concerning the issues and matters provided for in this agreement.

ARTICLE X
Modification

This Memorandum may not be changed or modified except in writing, signed by the party claiming such change or modification.

ARTICLE XI
Governing Law

This Memorandum shall be governed by the laws of the State of New York unless at the time when its provisions are sought to be enforced both parties reside in some other state, in which event the laws of that state shall govern.

In Witness Whereof, the parties hereto have signed their hands and seals this —— day of July, 1972.

—————————————————

Donald Brown

—————————————————

Ina Jones

The idea of this kind of cut-and-dried advance planning by two people presumably in love may seem not only unlikely but preposterous. Certainly, it goes against the grain of our romantic matrimonial traditions.

The engagement period, moreover (if this discreet interval still exists), may not be the most propitious time for us to examine the role-playing we are envisioning, or the neurotic needs we hope to have satisfied. Imagine, if you can, the starring and starry-eyed pre-wedlock pair in movies or on television, plotting the terms of their relationship and projecting possible dooms.

Yet the concept of couples planning their future soon *after* their marriage, and certainly long before its demise threatens, should be no fantasy.

It might instead be salvation.

CHAPTER 3

Affairs

Thou shalt not kill. Thou shalt not steal. Thou shalt not covet thy neighbor's wife (nor her ass). Thou shalt not commit adultery.

In our present climate, killing is an hourly fact, stealing a political act (coveting and taking are synonymous), and adultery is considered by many to be as archaic as the sanctity it violates.

What comes naturally is natural for the natural man. To him (or her) guilt is a hang-up, self-control a drag, indulgence a civil right. The righteous may still thunder from pulpits, and God-fearing citizens compress their lips in abhorrence, but even the law is now powerless to restrain the open expression of man's instinctual nature. Long legal and religious suppression, in fact, of its healthier manifestations bears considerable responsibility for the explosion of its sicker ones. And among the healthier manifestations now recognized by students of man is the open acceptance of sex, not only within but outside of marriage, as an essential human expression as well as need.

The reason for this preamble is that although extramarital affairs have existed in Western civilization, at least since recorded time, neither state, church, nor society has ever condoned them. Since these institutions were (and most still are) male-dominated, the burden of sin lay far more heavily on the adulteress than the adulterer. They might call him cad, rake, lecher, or rogue, but the smack of envy or admiration lay on the tongue. The woman caught in adultery was a thing of shame, defiled.

In this country, the laws of most states still punish her, and society still reserves the word "promiscuous" for women, not men. Church, state, and the majority of citizens still believe that marriage requires monogamy as the basis of family (and individual) health and morality, even though every form of mass communication in print or film or on the air records the gamut of unfettered sex—both within and without the confines of wedlock.

What they seldom record is the good marriage that still exists as evidence of a mutual love which usually includes but can also transcend sex. To be sure, this kind of marriage hardly makes for lively film or fiction. In the openly sensual climate of today we are led to believe that sexual incompatibility, absence of marital sex, or adultery are the rocks on which marriage founders. In reality, these factors rank, as causes for divorce, below matters of money, temperamental incompatibility, unions formed by the immature or those prolonged far beyond their natural death.

What we also find hard to believe is the surprising number of happy marriages in which the sexual needs of both partners are so slight that their satisfactions of companionship and mutual interests are sufficient fulfillment. Equally feasible are marriages in which the more demanding sexual partner finds outlets in periodic casual engagements which, through discretion or candor, do not erode the core of an otherwise happy family union.

Though society still frowns on such "flings" and the law still defines them as adultery, reputable authorities in the field of marriage and sex have in recent years stated publicly that such brief aberrances can benefit a marriage by relieving the tensions caused by unequal sexual drives or the tedium endured by one or the other. The alternatives of breaking up a marriage otherwise satisfying to both, or of enduring crippling self-denial, seem hardly preferable. Since sexual fulfillment for women as well as men has joined mass education as a prime human right (the Pursuit of Happiness?), the techniques, along with the sanction, of this pursuit have often submerged and neglected the essential meaning of love between human beings.

The cornerstone of this meaning is that exclusive intimacy of man and wife called monogamy, each one the sole possessor and possessed. To most mature and loving husbands and wives, the thought of the other in another's arms is a stab of pain and fear. Right or wrong, this sense of exclusive possession is still a deep human need.

Technically, one might argue that the smallest betrayal (the casual fling, the occasional one-night stand) is still treason. In human experience, however, the "affair" is the real and tangible danger to marriage.

For the difference between a "fling" and an "affair" is a matter of time, intensity, and involvement. The one is short-term and ephemeral: the other usually protracted and, inevitably, divisive. Paradoxically, nothing—in all the current loosening of mores and attitudes—has changed the basic emotional parabola of the extramarital affair.

The overriding reason for starting an affair in the first place is the same for men and women—the need for self-assurance as a desired and desiring human being. Good marriages supply this, in countless ways small and large. But when a husband and wife, through insensitivity or neglect, fail to give each other this assurance, they either resign themselves to frustration or tedium, or seek it elsewhere.

But what starts as a diversion or release or rapture regularly enjoyed can in time become a shadow-marriage, with all the mutual accommodations and conflicts that any prolonged human involvement demands. Like marriage, too, it rests on assumptions of long-term mutual desire and satisfactions that are more often unrealistic than not.

When these assumptions are not fulfilled, the affair can be kept alive only by "events" or "happenings"—the risk of disclosure, the techniques of secrecy, the near-escapes, the "special" restaurant, the emotional scenes, the guarded calls, the coded signals. The climate of crisis is the respirator, breathing life into waning desire, substituting emotional for sexual tension, and, finally, obliterating the release which the affair first provided.

At this point, the urge of the husband-lover to tell his wife (or vice versa) may become overwhelming. The conflict between his rival lives grows unbearable, his need for some sort of expiation or resolution imperative. Not because he wants a divorce, not because he wants to marry his mistress, but because the affair has outgrown its usefulness and negated his needs.

It is also precisely the time when honesty is a disastrous policy. His wife may forgive, but she will never forget. He may break off his affair completely, but any untoward action or evasion on his part, however innocent, may make her suspect new infidelities. The married pattern might continue as before, but the fabric has shredded.

You will notice that the instigator of this affair is the male, and that the woman married to him may forgive him for it.

It is the very rare husband, on the other hand, who would forgive his wife's transgressions, small or large, brief or extended. Most men would still be outraged or repelled by the acceptance of this freedom in their wives. That women married to them should also need occasional relief from tensions and tedium through intimacies, however casual, with others, is a threat to their ego: an ego long sustained by the myth of female passivity and lesser sexual drive. This myth they may have to relinquish, both in the case of wives and mistresses, as the functions of child-bearing and housekeeping in the former or careers in either no longer mute their female needs, if these are unmet by their mates.

Yet men will have the edge in one area, at least. After forty or fifty or sixty, the need and urge for sexual renewal may be equal in men and women, but a natural imbalance makes it far easier for men to attain it than women. Until their sixties men with waning sexual powers can attract most women they want, of whatever age. After their forties, women with sex drives no longer checked or reduced by involvement with children and housekeeping are lucky to find lovers, let alone husbands. They are particular victims of a mass-produced obsession with youth as the only prerequisite for love and desire. It is assumed that women over fifty cannot be ardent, loving, sexually imaginative, and physically attractive. And nothing in our culture—from clothes to literature—presents them as such. This loss is not only theirs, it is humanity's.

It is also a potent factor in the dissolution of marriages that were good enough to last, in mutual contentment, for twenty or more years. At this point the male fear of losing his sexual powers (i.e., his ego) peaks, driving him to some willing female half his age to restore them—and it.

This does not mean that he lives happily ever after, though marriages of men to women the age of their daughters are increasingly prevalent and often successful.

Yet to many a man, the urge to renewal repeats itself over and over, as familiarity with one nymphet breeds exhaustion or tedium, and he must move to the next for further proof of virility. Whether this charade is preferable to the lonely existence that thousands of women his age lead, can be argued if not resolved.

What cannot be argued is that the older man has a second, third, or even fourth chance for an intimate union while the older woman, with few exceptions, is offered none.

Unless, of course, the price of her husband's freedom to feel young is financial security for the rest of her life, and possibly someone to love her for her money if not her charms.

In this country, at least, the wistful fiction (based on Gallic fact) of the aging mistress surrounded by ardent young lovers remains fiction.

And so does the concept of affairs as being useful to a viable, if unexciting, marriage. Affairs are still—to put it lightly— serious risks. And truly loving married partners must know that restraint from this particular indulgence is part of their contract of trust—the main pillar of their union.

CHAPTER 4

The Array of Experts

Once divorce is seriously considered as a solution to marital strife, "expert" advice overabounds. If either mate has made up his mind, of course, then lawyers will be consulted. What kind of lawyer and why will be discussed later. Before that step, we turn to other sources of advice and comfort—very often, and often unwisely.

The first point to understand about experts is that there may not be time to profit from their skills. Once either mate has chosen a lawyer, the other *must* instantly consult a lawyer of his own. Preliminary legal maneuvers in the divorce process are often crucial, and the ability of a lawyer and his client to take advantage of a mate who either doesn't realize divorce is in the air, or, knowing it is, has chosen to consult his Yoga teacher, is awesome, as we shall discover.

Experts on divorce may be classified as: (a) lawyers; (b) the aiding professions such as psychiatrists, medical doctors, marriage counselors, members of the clergy; (c) the self-appointed, well-meaning friends who have been through it, and parade emotional scars and empty bank accounts as proof of their expertise; and (d) those we anoint as experts, such as business associates and, alas, our families.

Warning you about the hazards of (c) and (d) should be superfluous. Friends and relations may know us, but they rarely know our marriage. They may be important to us for support and sympathy, but their advice on how to get a divorce and whom to rely on is hardly any better than our own. If one swallow (or three, four, or five swallows) does not a summer make, neither do two, three, or four divorces an expert make.

There is very often little time to waste when divorce is a serious possibility. Marriages floundering on fragile ground are sometimes fatally affected by the unproductive emotional drain to which we subject ourselves at the hands of well-meaning novices. "I told you so." "My husband did the same thing and I couldn't take it." "My wife plays around a bit but so do I." "Honey, he's a man and all men act like that." "If she was my wife, I wouldn't take it." "What you need is a real son-of-a-bitch for a lawyer." "Anyone who could treat you like that deserves to be punished." "Do you want me to go talk to her?" All these and hundreds of similar forms of "advice" have ruined more marriages than they have saved. So have women friends of the wife, prone, inevitably, to gang up against "that man."

The risk that our friends will say something constructive is simply not worth taking. While we all grumble about our spouses to our closest friends and relatives, let us expect from them understanding rather than guidance.

How about the family G.P. or internist? The chances are that he knows very little about the process of diagnosing sick marriages or aiding (except unwittingly) their termination. Doctors are hard put enough to keep up with developments in their own profession without following new techniques in the divorce process. And although there is a first-rate medical journal (*Medical Aspects of Human Sexuality*) dealing with every phase of divorce, with heavy emphasis on the sexual problems of marriage, we suspect that very few doctors have time for it. Indeed, many articles in the journal clearly state that most physicians have neither the time nor skill to be of real primary assistance. Where the passions and rigors of marital discord cause severe medical problems, doctors are obviously necessary. Where the problems are less severe, internists who dispense sleeping pills and tran-

quilizers are often simply prlonging the anguish for their patients. Heavily sedated antagonists lack judgment, tend to vas-
cillate excessively, and often find the medical attention so
gratifying that the real problems are evaded till they erupt
again and the cycle begins anew.

For most of the sexual problems leading to the decisions to divorce, we tend to consult not only the G.P. and internist, but
the gynecologist and urologist. The pity of it is that, barring
specific psychological dysfunctions, none of these specialists
have the time or knowledge necessary to repair lost passions or
restore excitement or desire to marriage.

Where the marital problem is the familiar but often fatal "pre-
mature orgasm"–"lack of spontaneous orgasm"–"frigidity" con-
stellation, helpful information now abounds. Many doctors, be-
side Masters and Johnson, are working in this field, and you
may have the luck to find one.

But we assure you that the literature available to the public
in the crucial area of marriage, sex, and divorce varies from the
sickeningly inept to the moderately unhelpful.

Marriage and sex manuals too often set arbitrary norms and
confidently offer banal bromides which, when followed without
producing the promised fulfillment and rapture, can only make
the reader more doubtful concerning his or her capacity and
performance as a sexual partner. The manual is used by husband or wife as a bible of connubial bliss, an artificial standard
against which to measure the other's deficiencies.

And what of the psychiatrists and lay analysts? There is no
evidence at all that either group possesses any special knowledge in the field of marital and sexual counseling. Their training
is primarily directed toward the treatment of mental disease and
is geared toward helping a single patient, through drug, psy-
choanalytic, and group therapy, to function better as an individual. Nor is there any evidence that psychiatrists, analysts, or
psychologists make better husbands or wives or have less hang-
ups themselves about sex than their married patients.

The whole field of psychiatry and group therapy is presently in the throes of massive revolution, and married couples might well lose their way in the bewildering line-up of new psychiatric schools, attitudes, and techniques.

But all such therapy seems to us to be highly unresponsive to a genuine marital crisis. When the fangs have been bared and the knives unsheathed, discussions of toilet training, masturbation, and the childhood history of the patient, which are so useful in long-term analytic treatment, provide small help to a man or woman in desperate need of answers rather than questions.

Here also we can distinguish between the merely "disturbed" spouse and the one who is so emotionally and mentally crippled by his union that he requires immediate psychiatric help to face his problems. A spouse contemplating suicide over the destruction of marriage, or one who cannot function as a result of it, may require prolonged analysis—indeed, hospitalization. But it must be recognized that what is being treated are the symptoms of mental disease rather than the roots of marital discord.

Many couples in trouble consult marriage counselors. Unlike psychiatrists, most marriage counselors believe that in order to be of real value they must treat both husband and wife together. Significantly, this counseling concentrates on the immediate crisis, works backward, and seeks to give the partners a better insight into their mutual grievances. But serving both is at best hazardous.

Perhaps, more significantly, counseling depends upon the mutual effort of couples not yet so deeply immersed in crisis that they cannot face the demons together. For such a couple, there remains at least a spirit of cooperation and a willingness to endure the pain of self-revelation, even if other essential ingredients of the union are waning or in eclipse. As with psychiatry, there are no hard statistics available showing the extent of success or failure of the aiding profession devoted to resolving marital discord. Nor is it justifiable to assume that a couple who have "saved their marriage" through marriage counseling might not have saved it by themselves, or by other means.

As it is, there are countless lawyers, doctors, analysts, and marriage counselors who happily proclaim their success in saving marriages which are later either dissolved without their knowledge, or which continue to subsist in such a troubled state that the temporary respite afforded by the "cure" was scarcely worth the effort and expense.

Unhappily, we conclude that choosing marital experts is at best a gamble and that several factors unrelated to the field of expertise chosen are more significant:

(a) At what period of the crisis does either or both of the spouses consult an expert?

(b) Can the real crisis be properly identified, articulated, appreciated, and solved?

(c) Is the motivation of both spouses, at the time the crisis is dealt with, sufficient to produce effective results?

(d) Did the expert or experts consulted possess the knowledge, skill, and empathy to diagnose and make creative suggestions concerning the particular marriage about which they are consulted, and were the parties receptive at that particular moment in their crisis?

One thing is certain: talk unaccompanied by a change in behavior never saved a single marriage. Marriages in crisis require these changes of one or both partners. Sometimes only one partner alone makes the necessary behavioral adjustment. Time, alone, tends to worsen things, and change of location by either or both partners gives, at most, temporary respite, and very often serves only to harden irreconcilable positions.

Unfortunate as it may seem, timing and luck play significant roles in the mending of ruptured marriages. If we are wise or lucky enough to recognize the necessity for change, either by ourselves or with the help of others, marriages in decline may rise, reach new levels, and go on to thrive. In the absence of luck and timing, the only alternative is to stop mourning what is lost and start building new lives, free of destructive memories and unworkable habit patterns.

Just as we must nurture a marriage in trouble and work to avoid possible crisis, we must be equally alert to recognize marriages wholly dependent upon crisis. Many husbands and wives lead tedious and unrewarding lives, in which one or both partners are forever creating upheavals—in order to avoid real confrontation and communication, in order to avoid sexual relationship no longer enjoyable or even endurable, in order to avoid the necessity of intellectual and emotional repair, and in order to avoid the realization that the marriage is truly over.

Finally, a word about newspapers as a source of matrimonial guidance. "Dear Abby" is a darling, but if you are so shallow that your problems can be solved in her column, this book is far too complicated for you.

More significant are the misinformation and misinterpretations filtered through newspaper accounts of matrimonial proceedings. Few matrimonial lawyers have escaped the indignant remonstrances of clients who want guarantees that their cases will or will not be luridly described in newspapers, or who wish to obtain the lavish settlements achieved by other lawyers whose names regularly appear in the press.

Matrimonial proceedings rarely attract the press unless the parties themselves are extremely well known or the case involves conduct far juicier than most of us can claim. Many, if not most, of the newspaper stories originate with lawyers who are friendly with a member of the press assigned to cover trials in major courts. Reliable rumor has it that such stories are hand-delivered by the lawyer or his client along with bottles of whisky or other coin of the realm. The reputations of lawyers described as "triumphant," "hard-fighting," "aggressive," "prominent," etc., are less the product of these sterling qualities than of unethical public-relations campaigns. Choosing a lawyer because his name appears in the press regularly is as intelligent as choosing a restaurant on the road because neon lights flash the words "Excellent Cuisine."

CHAPTER 5

Hiring Lawyers

The important questions concerning the hiring of lawyers are why, when, who, and how much. The answers to each are significant, far-reaching, and little understood by the public.

Obviously, the first question is: Do you need a lawyer, and for what purpose? One function a lawyer can perform is counseling. We have already questioned the advisability of engaging others for this purpose. The most favorable quality supposedly possessed by lawyers is their objectivity and their experience in resolving conflicts between parties at odds. They should, and often do, possess the ability to reduce what seems like endless warfare to the few essential disputes which, if resolved, might achieve harmony. This ability is possessed, or should be, by general practitioners, by corporate or commercial lawyers, by matrimonial lawyers, and even by other legal specialists. Again, however, there is no evidence that lawyers are any more happily married or any better adjusted sexually than other specialists. More importantly, most lawyers who are not familiar with matrimonial law have neither the time nor the inclination to get involved in the emotional entanglements of warring spouses. As a group, however, lawyers sometimes serve a useful function, very often unknown to themselves. Frequently, they are consulted simply to scare the other mate and to let him know that this time the dissatisfied spouse means business. More often than is supposed, the very act of consulting a lawyer has the desired effect.

It would seem logical that one should seriously consider consulting the so-called matrimonial specialist. He should be more knowledgeable than his colleagues in other specialties, not only in the laws and decisions that affect his client's rights, but also in sensing whether his client truly wants out, or wants to stay in —but under better conditions. Many matrimonial specialists serve that function extremely well, while others avoid it sedulously. Some feel unqualified for the role of "emotional adviser"; others feel they are too overworked to assume that role. Some may excel in protecting their client's rights in matrimonial negotiations, but make poor advisers. Curiously enough, some find the role of adviser easier when representing men, and some when representing women—depending upon their own particular married experience and on their matrimonial practice.

There simply is no one lawyer for everybody, no matter how knowledgeable the lawyer may be. The client should feel that he or she will receive not only the lawyer's legal skills but also, depending upon the matrimonial tension existing, the attorney's understanding and empathy.

This need for empathy is usually far greater when women employ lawyers. It is difficult for women to conceive matrimonial negotiations; they tend to see them as an extension of the unhappy marriage in which they are already the victim, downcast and browbeaten. They fear that their lawyer will be seduced by the husband's superior business knowledge or commercial fluency. They fear that their lawyer will be overpowered as are their husband's friends, business associates, employees, etc. Alone, or alone with her children and relatives, the wife's demons loom large and unconquerable, and she seeks the lawyer who, upon meeting, she decides can best stand up to the bully-husband. Untrained in selecting counsel and beset by fears, the chance of her choosing the right lawyer is frankly poor, and the choice often irrational. Many lawyers take advantage of what they sense are their female client's qualms and desires, and put on thundering office performances full of promises and fury, but in reality hollow. Many well-known lawyers, advertised as silver-tongued orators, become ineffectual Milquetoasts in a real courtroom.

Obviously, the usual reason for hiring a lawyer is simply because one or both of the parties desires to terminate the relationship. Once the decision has been made, the question is: Who can best protect the client?

How does one go about selecting a lawyer? The best source is most likely to be another lawyer, since even lawyers who do not undertake matrimonial work are frequently called upon to recommend competent lawyers who do. Through their associations and memberships in various bar associations they are likely to know who the competent experts are. If a prospective client knows no lawyers, another excellent source of information would be the various city and state bar associations, or the office of the American Academy of Matrimonial Lawyers, whose membership is national. Many recommendations, of course, are made by family and friends, but such recommendations have obvious weaknesses. That a lawyer comes highly recommended is significant, but should not be conclusive. Contrary to widespread belief, lawyers are people. Their personalities, temperaments, senses of humor, and intellectual accomplishments vary considerably and so do their backgrounds. There must be some mutuality of expectations and goals between the lawyer and the client. A lawyer unsympathetic to his client's position would obviously be a poor advocate of it. After conferring, there must be some accommodation of views, or the relationship is likely to be a poor one.

Curious as it may seem, many lawyers who are extremely effective when representing husbands, do very poorly when representing wives—and the reverse is equally true. A thrice-married lawyer paying significant amounts of alimony is likely to be less sympathetic to a woman's cause than a lawyer with a more fortunate marital background. A happily married lawyer whose wife put him through law school might obviously be less sympathetic to a husband hoping to opt out of all of his marital obligations. Client or lawyer may simply dislike each other. Under those circumstances the lawyer's reputation or high recommendation does not justify the client's confidence.

Although it is essential that both lawyer and client respect each other, and that the former be sympathetic to the pain and distress of the latter, the lawyer need not be, or should he be, "some kind of an executioner of a spouse's wrath and vengeance," as Mitchell Salem Fisher, a distinguished matrimonial attorney, has said. It is not the lawyer's function to be a father-substitute, nor is it advisable or helpful for him to becloud his own judgment in the matrimonial turbulence he is engaged to terminate. A lawyer who undertakes to seek what his client wants rather than what is fair and reasonably attainable under the law is a fraud; he is undertaking a cruel hoax and perpetuating, rather than solving, marital discord.

Early on, clients must be disabused of either a lawyer's or a court's responsibility to punish or avenge past marital transgressions, except and to the extent that the law permits. It is after all the client and not the lawyer or the court who married the offending spouse, and the expectation, desire, or obsession of some clients that the lawyer require penance for the wrongs done them is unreasonable and unhelpful.

Lawyers representing wives have an obligation to use all the skills of their advocacy to attain for them and their children the maximum support at the least cost economically and emotionally. This does not include an obligation to leave a husband destitute—unable to support a new mate or to lead a new life. A lawyer representing a husband is obliged to make certain that his client after divorce or separation can lead a fruitful life without being obligated to work solely for a family no longer his. That obligation does not embrace a duty to leave wife and children destitute and without sufficient support to manage for themselves. We consider later the process by which a lawyer attempts to protect his client's rights. But we emphasize that lawyers owe no obligation to their clients to be either rogues on behalf of husbands or overreaching advocates on behalf of wives.

A client should do all he or she can do to hire an effective advocate without expecting an accomplice in hatred.

How much of a lawyer's time does a client buy when he retains him? As much (although many lawyers do not agree) as is reasonably required. Marital discord ranges from the very amiable to the excruciatingly acrimonious. A lawyer who does not answer or return telephone calls, who impatiently hangs up on his clients, or who is continually inaccessible during evening hours is very often useless to a client. Late evening marital turbulence happens more and more frequently because of lawyers' strategy, some courts' philosophy, and because of the economic necessity that compels many separating or divorcing spouses to live together under the same roof during the divorce process. Thus their worst clashes and their most profound anxieties are bound to occur when they are together—usually during the evening. The lawyer or his associate must be available when he is needed.

This by no means implies that he must give his heart and personal life over to his clients. He does not, and should not, become another combatant. He does not, and should not, become a referee in the endless quarreling and bickering that so often accompany the divorce process. The client must be willing to learn that the lawyer is unable to intervene, or even to be helpful, in most of the squabbling that follows the decision to divorce. He cannot stop the husband from smoking cigars in order to annoy the wife. He cannot compel the wife to make the husband's bed or launder his shirts. He should not be hauled into the arena every time one partner threatens the other with economic ruination or with the familiar, "My lawyer will kill your lawyer."

But where, for example, a husband threatens serious physical harm to his wife or children, or where the wife arrives home with thousands of dollars of expensive and superfluous merchandise, or where the police are called to protect a beaten or threatened spouse or because one or the other mate is trying to "make a case," the spouse has a right to know what he or she should do, and the lawyer presiding over the equitable termination of a marriage and being paid for it should not consider the client's call an imposition.

Every lawyer experienced in matrimonial litigation has met the impossible client: the woman (less frequently, the man) whose calls are endless, fatuous, and solely concerned with personal loneliness or bitterness. If a client will not or cannot understand that the line between the important and the trivial must be drawn, the relationship with the lawyer must be terminated, or the lawyer must somehow endure. But surely it is not his legal or ethical responsibility to give over his law practice and his personal life to a pest.

One thing is sure: clients must be taught to accept as nonsense statements such as: "My lawyer is better than your lawyer," "My lawyer says you won't get a dime," and "My lawyer says when he gets through with you, you won't have a dime left." In the first place, the client is usually misquoting the lawyer, and, in the second place, any lawyer who makes such statements is usually a pushover. The threat, more often than not, is good news rather than bad news since saber-rattling blowhards tend to make very bad lawyers.

A recurring theme of this book is the astounding inability of spouses in strife to comprehend that, except with respect to matters of custody, the efforts of the court and of the lawyers should be concerned mainly with how equitably to divide assets and income. And although in many states it is said that neither party has any vested right in the assets of the other, the existence of such assets plays a significant role in matrimonial negotiations and in court decisions, regardless of the law on the books.

Accordingly, only the very rich are relatively unaffected by the diminution in assets or income caused by the payment of either party's legal fees. If less solvent couples, however, would realize how significant such diminutions might be to them, they could come to terms with the heavy price of bickering and quarreling not only in money but in the emotional damage of matrimonial litigation.

Husbands are expected to pay their attorneys a retainer in advance and the balance depending upon such ambiguous criteria as the number of hours spent, the lawyer's normal hourly rate, the lawyer's standing in the community, the difficulty encountered by the lawyer either because of the novelty of the law applicable or the unusual number of factual disputes that must be resolved, the results achieved, the husband's wealth and income, or some combination of those factors. The rich pay more, the comfortable pay a lot (but a lot less), and the poor pay significantly less (although they may have considerable difficulty in hiring the lawyer they would like). Where very little income or assets are involved, the suffering may be no different than for the affluent, but the amount of legal work is much less.

Wives with their own money are, like their husbands, expected to pay their lawyers a retainer in advance. And if the lawyer finds these assets considerable, he may demand a fee based on the same criteria used for the husband.

If she has neither assets nor income enough to pay whatever retainer is agreed upon, the lawyer has to rely on the court or settlement negotiations for payment.

The attitudes of the courts vary, from state to state and from community to community, concerning the value of services rendered for matrimonial cases. Some courts regard matrimonial matters as bothersome nuisances and hold matrimonial specialists in low esteem. In those states and communities, a lawyer is loath to rely upon the court's largesse and tends to insist upon the wife making arrangements to pay his fees at least up to some set amount.

The plain fact is that very few matrimonial specialists have become judges, and lawyers tend to receive larger fees in settlements than they do in court. Indeed, the lure of large fees to wives' lawyers has probably led to many unfortunate settlements for the wives represented because of the conscious and unconscious anxiety on the part of the wife's lawyer that the court, which fixes the fee for the wife's lawyer, would direct a lesser counsel fee than might accrue from a settlement negotiation.

For obvious reasons, it is unethical and improper for a wife's lawyer to discuss his fees or to permit their discussion until all of the essential terms of a settlement are agreed to in advance. It is correspondingly improper for a husband's lawyer to enter into such discussions prematurely.

One of the questions frequently asked of lawyers is why they request payment in advance. The answer is that experience has taught them that too many couples, ever-dependent on them when the fury raged, suddenly reconcile. And when the bloom is back on the marital rose, the couple conveniently remembers only how unhelpful or inflammatory the lawyer's presence was. Some couples seem to spend most of their married lives in litigation, going from lawyer to lawyer, but always stopping short of a court trial. Something about their fear of the courtrooms (TV conditioning?) drives them into sudden mutual forgiveness and realliance, and the united front they then present to their lawyers, who end up having to sue for their fees, is something the lawyers try to guard against.

Mr. and Mrs. X had been married over twenty years, had four lovely children, an apartment in New York, and a house in the suburbs. She was at one time a well-known theatrical personality and her husband a well-known musician. After years of recurring marital explosions, they indulged in some bizarre behavior. The husband began removing property from the apartment, threatening and verbally taunting the wife, and she, in turn, one hot summer day, stabbed him several times with a kitchen knife. The husband promptly charged the wife with assault, and the proceeding was brought to the Family Court of the City of New York. The wife's attorney took the position that since there were already matrimonial proceedings for separation in which each party was countersuing the other in the Supreme Court, the Family Court lacked jurisdiction. The Family Court asked for memoranda of law and adjourned the case. After the submission of such memoranda the court notified the parties' attorneys that it would not dismiss the petition on jurisdictional grounds, and proceeded to try the case. After the trial, the court held that the wife had been provoked by her husband and dismissed the petition.

The husband stopped supporting the wife and gave each of the children the most minimal sum; the wife proceeded to make an application for temporary alimony and counsel fees. The husband said, in opposition to that motion, that he was so mentally disturbed as a result of the various lawsuits and the matrimonial acrimony that he was unable to continue working, and that musicians were finding it increasingly difficult to find employment in New York and were all heading west. The wife's lawyer triumphantly produced records, filed by the husband over twenty years previously in connection with the husband's first marriage, in which he had made the exact same claims concerning his imminent breakdown, his poor physical condition, and the status of musicians in New York. While the motion was being decided, the court and the wife's counsel received a letter from a New York hospital that the husband was indeed being treated with shock therapy, that he was seriously disturbed mentally, and that his future as a musician was impaired for the foreseeable future. The court denied the wife's application.

As the case proceeded to reach trial in early summer, the wife became increasingly hysterical and was herself hospitalized for various physical and mental ailments.

On the eve of trial (the husband having miraculously regained his composure and mental stability), the wife found herself unable to go to court. She kept calling her lawyer, as did her doctor and her relatives, pleading for one adjournment after another because she could not endure a whole summer not knowing what her economic future would be. (The courts are very often closed for trials during the summer.) The court, heeding the pleas of the wife's counsel and sympathetic to the contention that the welfare of minor children was involved, put the case over to the last trial date before summer recess.

On that date, the husband's lawyer came into court (for the first time without his client), walked up to the wife's lawyer and said, "You son-of-a-bitch, are you responsible for this?" and showed him a letter from his client firing him. The wife's lawyer broke out laughing and showed the husband's lawyer the exact same letter which he had received from *his* client.

Somehow, Mr. and Mrs. Show Biz had managed to reconcile and had engaged another lawyer for the sole purpose of firing the two lawyers who had been representing them in the three proceedings which they had been involved in.

Several years later the couple resumed their litigious ways and the wife had the gall to come to her former lawyer again and ask to be represented. The lawyer had enough sense to require his entire fee in advance, which was willingly paid, but he also had a very clear memory of the torment he would have to go through representing this lady again.

Frequently, also, married couples in the divorce process run amok and dissipate their assets to a point where there is nothing left for the lawyer. And, quite naturally, lawyers are often unable to achieve the unrealistic expectations of their clients. Lawyers are unwilling to have their fees depend on what their clients think they should receive after the marital struggle is over.

Consider, for example, the couple who go through their lives lavishly spending more money than they earn. They have two cars, two poodles, a maid, and a summer place, and their increasing debt is ignored year after year. Finally, when the divorce process begins and the lawyers and accountants shudder at the economic disaster before them, the wife simply cannot get used to the fact that the judge did not make appropriate allowance for poodle-clipping or gardening. Furious, she points out to her lawyer that her next door neighbor fared far better with Lawyer X and she could not understand why her Lawyer Y should be paid anything. It is also fascinating to consider how many clients are willing to go into debt to maintain their yacht, dogs, and polo ponies, but who indignantly say to their lawyers,

"You know my real financial condition—I am broke." Lawyers are singularly unmoved by such claims when they negotiate fees.

Surely a useful rule to remember is that the agreement concerning fees should be discussed with the lawyer, should be understood by both parties, and should be put in writing. Women who think that "since my husband is paying for it, I don't care" are making a foolish mistake. She is paying for it, too.

The question is frequently asked whether women lawyers should be hired to represent husbands and wives in divorce proceedings. There are many prominent matrimonial specialists who are women, and whose virtuosity is unquestioned. It is assumed that they will be more sympathetic to a woman's point of view, but this is often not the case. They are, after all, women who are highly motivated or used to competing with men, sometimes inclined, moreover, to look down at their less independent sisters whose lives as housewives they regard with little respect. Apart from this, the same criteria for hiring lawyers generally should be applied to women as to men, with the further reservation that few women lawyers excel in trial work in this country as they do, for example, in France and Sweden. This is partially due to the "male chauvinism" frequently and justly observed by current writers, and it may also be attributable to the massive courtrooms, which abound in the United States, in which the female voice does not carry very well. It is difficult sometimes for women lawyers to retain both the femininity expected by American judges and male colleagues, and to assert their advocacy in a system administered and inhabited mostly by men. Few women, and no honest men in any profession, can deny that this double burden exists in what is still, if decreasingly, a man's world.

CHAPTER 6

The Goals and Strategies of Matrimonial Warfare

Apart from questions concerning the custody of children, the only realistic goals of a separation or divorce are freedom and the division of the economic spoils. For husband or wife, how to get his or her fair share is the question at hand. Different kinds of couples, naturally, have different goals, which may be classified as follows:

(a) THE EXCEPTIONAL COUPLE: They realize the marriage is over; they each wish to pursue their independent lives; they each wish to have equitable provisions made for support of the wife and children, and they wish to do it as quickly and amiably as possible.

(b) THE AVERAGE COUPLE: They each wish to fix alimony for the wife and support for the children in accordance with how they assess the blame for the breakup of the marriage; each sees himself as a victim and wishes retribution, revenge, and monetary compensation.

(c) THE BITTERLY MILITANT COMBATANTS: They each want blood and each wants to ruin the other. The husband wants to leave the wife and children as nearly penniless as possible. The wife's goal is to destroy her husband, his reputation, his business, his friendships, his relation with his children, without regard to her own personal consequences.

Variations abound, of course, since a husband may belong to

53

one of the above classifications and his wife to another. He may
be a militant and she a peacemaker. It is even possible, and not
altogether rare, that the reasonable couple, in good faith, hire
lawyers who become the combatants, turning what could be a
quick and equitable settlement into prolonged matrimonial
havoc.

But the real issue is money and property. If the day ever
comes when either marital partner desiring a divorce can acti-
vate a computer and have made available to him, to his spouse,
and to their advisers a true, detailed, and analytic financial
statement of the joint income and joint assets and liabilities of
the parties, divorce proceedings would be foreshortened, and
the pain and anguish diminished beyond the imaginable powers
of our legislators, marriage-manual experts, lawyers, and judges.
That single computerized financial statement handed to the
marital combatants and their advisers is really what divorce
proceedings are all about. Its possession by the lawyers, the accountants, and the judges would short-circuit the lies, the eva-
sions, the duplicity, and most of the acrimony that mark marital
litigation—from the earliest conference between lawyers to right
up to the trial.

As we shall see, an able attorney for the wife must be a combination psychiatrist, detective, and bookkeeper.

A husband's lawyer, where possible, produces and directs
a script portraying his client as a victim whose assets and income are on the decline, whose life is waning, whose spirit has
been drained by years of nagging and overreaching, and whose
future portends financial decline, loneliness, uncertainty, and
depression. Within the law he must thwart the wife's counsel in
the search for assets and income. He must explain away whatever is found and must convince the court that whatever is discovered is more securely held, for the benefit of the children, by
his more businesslike and sensible client than by the extrava-
gant and less commercially oriented woman, who will only
dissipate what she gets.

In other words, the husband's counsel attempts to attribute to the wife all of the characteristics of the "alimony drone" condemned by Judge Samuel H. Hofstadter—a woman intent on continuing or embarking on the responsibility-free life of indolence; a woman effortlessly maintaining an unproductive existence at the expense of a husband struggling to embark upon a new life. The wife's counsel, on the other hand, attempts to picture the husband as a man abundantly able to continue supporting her and her children in the style to which he has induced them to become accustomed, and which he is well able to continue providing—despite whatever innovative protestations of the husband's lawyer that "now that love has gone," so has the means to support the family.

The nauseating lengths to which spouses go to exaggerate their claims are reported in decision after decision, from court after court, in state after state.

For example, in one case reported in New York, to use the court's words:

Eight hundred and eighty-four pages of testimony deal exclusively with the conflicting claims of the parties with respect to their standard of living prior to the institution of this action and as to the true financial status of the defendant. The entire eight trial days were devoted to testimony by the plaintiff, her sister, and a brother-in-law, which painted a glowing picture of exceedingly sumptuous living which included the occupancy of a twenty-five-room mansion situated on five stately acres with improved outbuildings and pool; membership in an exclusive country club, winter vacations in Florida; incidental trips to Las Vegas, the Catskills, and Greenbrier; expensive summer camps for the children, college tuition; unlimited charge accounts in all of the "Fifth Avenue" shops; and to testimony of the defendant and his accountant, which tended to portray the defendant as a hard-working businessman operating three separate corporations owned by him while, at the same time, imploring the plaintiff to control her extravagances, pointing out to her that they were living on a scale far in excess of that commensurate with his income. Not surprisingly, the pictures painted were as incompatible and as much at variance as is pop art with an old master.

The plaintiff testified at length respecting the amounts previously spent, in great detail, and the total of such expenditures, if accurate, exceeded $100,000 per year. She claimed that approximately one-half of all household and family expenses were charged against one or more of the defendant's corporations, and were paid for by checks of said corporations. For example, the plaintiff testified that after their present home was purchased for some $115,000, it was renovated and furnished at a cost of $34,000, which was paid for by check of Val Mode Lingerie, Inc., one of defendant's wholly owned corporations, and, when she questioned the defendant about this, he allegedly told her this would be charged by the corporation to refurbishing its showrooms. Thereafter, the plaintiff averred, the wages of the household domestic help amounting to $7000 per year, the gardener's charges amounting to $2400 per year, home entertaining by caterers amounting to several thousands of dollars per year, winter vacations costing $2500, country-club charges of $3500 per year, and many other purely personal family expenses were charged to one of the defendant's corporations and paid for by corporate checks. Some of the major items, said the plaintiff, were various charge accounts maintained by her which amounted to more than $30,000 per year. She further swore that in addition to an open charge account maintained at Saks Fifth Avenue, each year the defendant purchased $20,000 worth of gift certificates with corporate checks from that store, which he gave to her to spend. The defendant, on the other hand, testified and offered canceled checks in substantiation, that his corporation purchased an average of $5500 worth of gift certificates over the past five years which were given to its customers. The defendant further testified that each year about 10 or 15 per cent of these certificates were refused by customers ($550 to $825) and these he would give to the plaintiff to spend. The defendant also offered in evidence copies of his federal income-tax returns for the past five years, which showed an average net income of about $26,000. However, in view of the proof offered, undisputed in many instances, that the defendant used funds of his corporations indiscriminately to pay personal charges which clearly had no relationship to legitimate corporate expense, his personal income-tax returns do not truly reflect his income (*Gladstone* v. *Gladstone,* 35 Misc. 2d 206; *Stahl* v. *Stahl,* 221 N.Y.S. 2d 931; amended 16 A.D. 2d 467). Copies of the tax returns of the defendant's corporations were also introduced in evidence. The accuracy of these returns is also questionable as to how much personal expense is buried in "travel and entertaining," "personal services," etc. For example, the defendant admits paying his mother $100 per week by corporate check, although she renders no service to the corporation. He also admitted charging his own vacation expense and the cost of meats consumed in his home to corporate "travel and entertaining." If all of these illegitimate charges were ferreted out and disallowed the corporate profits would be considerably higher which would, in turn, be reflected in higher actual earnings of the defendant.

We find incredible the plaintiff's testimony that the defendant bought and gave her $20,000 in Saks gift certificates while, at the same time, maintaining an open charge account at the same store against which she charged purchases aggregating an additional $4000 per year. The defendant's version is more believable, i.e., that he permitted the plaintiff to have open charge accounts and that the only gift certificates he gave her were the small amounts rejected by his business buyers. We believe that both parties exaggerated; the plaintiff by professing larger expenditures than were actually made, and the defendant by seeking to minimize them. Even assuming the defendant's version to be more nearly correct, his proof indicates a scale of living of approximately $60,000 per year, of which $15,000 was necessary to pay carrying charges, repairs, and maintenance of the house, plus $7000 more for domestic help and gardeners. He had been giving the plaintiff $9400 per year in cash for food, excluding eggs, butter, and milk. Tuition cost him $4000 a year; country-club expenses $2500 per year; his mother $5700 per year; children's camps $2400; charges at Saks alone $3500; other charge accounts; the maintenance of two automobiles; entertaining; vacations; etc. This, of course, is far in excess of the defendant's income, as reflected by his income-tax returns, and is mute testimony as to their unreliability as a true indication of income.

After analyzing the testimony of both sides and the various exhibits offered in evidence in support thereof, and considering the fact that the defendant is the sole owner of three corporations (at least two of which are very profitable) whose profits he can declare as dividends to himself at will, the court is of the opinion that the plaintiff is entitled to receive for support and maintenance for herself and the unemancipated five children, the total sum of Six Hundred ($600.00) Dollars per week, allocated Two Hundred ($200.00) Dollars per week for alimony, and Four Hundred Dollars ($400.00) per week for support of the children, commencing one week from the date of entry of judgment. Out of the sum, which is intended to be exclusive, the plaintiff will be required to maintain a home and provide for all living expenses and luxuries for herself and the children. It is strongly urged that the present residence be sold. The purchase of a more modest home will substantially enhance the financial position of plaintiff.

The plaintiff and the children are awarded exclusive possession of the marital residence in Purchase, N.Y., with the understanding that its entire expense and maintenance is to be borne solely by the plaintiff.

In addition, plaintiff is awarded counsel fees, over and above any sums previously awarded, in the sum of $10,000.00, which is to include all expenditures of plaintiff's counsel in the preparation and trial of this action, with the exception of taxable disbursements.

Imagine a court in the name of justice awarding more income for the support of the wife and children than the husband and his counsel were willing to concede he earned in an entire year! Just as numerous are the cases where wives seek support for themselves and the children in amounts which they and their counsel know, or should know, exceed more than the husband ever earned in any year of his life.

Nor are the exaggerations restricted to the carriage trade. In another New York case, the wife sought to hold her husband in contempt of court for his refusal to abide by a judgment of separation which had directed the husband to pay plaintiff $100 weekly for her support and for the support of a two-and-a-half-year-old daughter. The defendant sought a modification downward of his obligation on the grounds of a "substantial reduction in his income since the entry of judgment." The court in attempting to resolve the conflicting contentions of the parties said as follows:

> The sum and substance of the hearing established that until judgment in the separation action, the husband was a foreman in an automobile body-repair shop who steadily averaged $300 per week in salary and commissions.
>
> All the witnesses agreed that defendant is a highly skilled auto-body repairman, [that] men of such abilities are in scarce supply, and are very well paid.
>
> At any rate, no sooner had the judgment of separation been signed, when we find a recurrence of that not so strange phenomenon I alluded to in my opinion dated March 15, 1968 (*Siegel* v. *Siegel,* N.Y. L.J., p. 18, col. 1), wherein a successful man becomes an instant failure. The overnight metamorphosis of $300 per week man to $100 per week man is a by-product of his sudden firing, and singular hiring by a separated lady (who knows nothing about the auto-body repair business), to manage her newly incorporated auto-body repair shop. Defendant's new lady boss has problems of her own. She not only has three children by a husband who apparently is not supporting her, but is also the mother of a three-week-old infant fathered by the defendant herein.
>
> While the court commiserates with the parties to this triangle, defendant's distressing situation is of his own making. His primary obligation is to his wife and child—although the court will not close its eyes to defendant's newly acquired responsibility.
>
> Under all the circumstances, the court decision is as follows:

Motion to punish granted. Defendant is fined the sum of the arrears. He may purge himself of the contempt by paying the fine at the rate of $20 per week in addition to current alimony.

Defendant's cross-motion to modify the judgment of separation is granted to the extent that weekly payments are reduced to $80 per week effective as of the return date of the cross-motion. Plaintiff is awarded a counsel fee in the sum of $150 for the instant proceedings payable at the rate of $50 per month commencing thirty days after service of a copy of the order to be entered hereon to be settled on notice.

It must be stressed that the divorce laws in this country vary radically from state to state. And even where different states have similar grounds for divorce such as cruelty, adultery, abandonment, habitual drunkenness, or others—the definition of those terms varies just as drastically from jurisdiction to jurisdiction. In some states what is sauce for the goose is not sauce for the gander, and the same behavior countenanced in men will not be countenanced in women. In Kentucky, for example, a wife may be granted a divorce if she can prove that her husband is "living in adultery" (as distinguished from having occasionally indulged in it), while the husband may be granted a divorce by proving that his wife is engaged in "lascivious behavior." What is cruelty in one state may not be considered such in another state recognizing the same grounds. Defenses such as provocation, condonation (forgiveness), recrimination (roughly meaning "Yeah, but you did something bad, too"), connivance ("You made me or induced me to do it"), and others, are similarly applied and defined very differently from state to state and in some jurisdictions are not applied at all, or are available only in defense of some grounds and not in defense of others.

The sovereignty of the state is slow to recognize the sovereignty of the individual in private relationships.

To one extent or another, most courts are given broad discretion in determining the amount of support to award to a guiltless wife and to her children. Depending upon the jurisdiction, the court may also be given broad discretion in determining whether and to what extent assets rather than income may be divided. In New York, for example, the court has no discretion in dividing personal or real property held in the name of either spouse individually. This is so, of course, provided the property came to be held individually by that spouse lawfully and not by trick, artifice, or overreaching; for example, where the husband has been depositing his wife's inheritance checks in his own account without her permission. New York courts, however, do have the power, within limits of discretion, to award possession of real property to either spouse regardless of ownership, pending trial, and to a much more limited extent after trial. Other states permit the court, within its discretion, to redistribute assets between the parties, and many community-property states presume joint ownership of property acquired by either party after marriage to be equally owned. But regardless of the rule of law to be applied, the amount of assets, real or personal, owned by the respective spouses is a very important consideration to a court in exercising its discretion as to the amount of support it will award as alimony for the wife and as support for the children.°

Another important consideration in determining the amount of support to be awarded or to be achieved by settlement is the whole notion of "fault." The guilt that a successful party in a divorce proceeding has to prove against the other varies in this country from none to a lot. We now have so-called "no-fault" jurisdictions (i.e., states) such as California, Florida, New Jersey, and other jurisdictions that have some "no-fault" grounds for divorces and separation, and other grounds which require fault. And there are many jurisdictions which will grant a divorce or

° It should be noted that in two states, Pennsylvania and Texas, permanent alimony may not be awarded by the court, the right to support being held to terminate with the dissolution of the marriage. In New Hampshire, alimony awards are limited to successive three-year periods where there are no children and it becomes progressively more difficult to persuade the court on the successive applications that alimony should be granted at all.

separation only upon proof of fault as defined by the legislatures of those various states. The same wife who might be denied any support at all because of her "guilt" under the laws of New York might be entitled to $1000 a week support in California.

In some states in which fault plays a part, the judge may have the right or legal authority to take the spouse's guilt into consideration, i.e., to make "the punishment fit the crime." Or, the law of the jurisdiction may simply say that once the crime has been committed no divorce or separation may be granted nor may the court award support to the guilty wife.° And in some states the judge may have the authority to order support depending on how "guilty" the offending spouse is. The net effect of these various grounds in different jurisdictions is predictable: the wives and husbands, their witnesses, and their attorneys simply set out to prove that real grounds exist, and where they don't, weave facts out of fantasy. The frantic urge for freedom breeds perjury, and the same exaggerations which abound in proving and disproving financial ability proliferate in accusations and denials of guilt.

It would be a tragic misuse of this book and a subversion of its intentions were the reader to attempt to become his own lawyer. Matrimonial law, while surely no more difficult to comprehend than other legal specialties, still cannot be grasped or even vaguely understood by the layman. And few lawyers make any pretense at being experts in the widely divergent matrimonial laws of each state. Dealing as we do here, however, with matrimonial strategy, and with its use and misuse in achieving the goals of divorcing parties, it is still important that a lawyer understand that knowledge of how the law for his client and against his or her adversary becomes an important tool. Before assessing, therefore, how the husband's lawyer and the wife's lawyer each proceeds to accomplish his client's goals, we might review the raw material which either uses in negotiating

---

° The same rule applies in those states where the husband may also be awarded support.

or litigating in his client's interest. The areas of marital combat are as follows:

(a) The conflicting contentions concerning whether "grounds" exist under the applicable law, and whether one party or the other is sufficiently guilty to satisfy legal requirements.

(b) The legitimate legal rules which apply to the facts of a given case. Lawyers argue interminably over whether their client's position is legally tenable or not. The prospective complaining party's lawyer maintains that, under the facts, he can prove his client is clearly entitled to prevail. The defending party's counsel says: "In the first place you can't prove it, and in the second place, even if you could you would not satisfy the legal requirements." He further maintains that even if the proof were accepted and were sufficient, his client has available to him or her various defenses which would defeat the plaintiff's claim. He goes further and says, "Not only can't you prove your case, but my client has a claim against your client"; and *"la ronde"* goes on.

(c) Whose client can better endure? Who has the necessary financial and emotional "staying power," the required ability to put up with the seemingly unending days, weeks, months, and even years (in rare cases, of course) of marital feuding?

(d) The financial flimflam previously referred to: WIFE: "I have been loyal, I have been good, I have been victimized, I am needy, he is rich." HUSBAND: "She is the wrong-doer, the tramp, and I am poor."

(e) A potpourri of other influences can be used by either party and, with questionable ethics, by his attorney. The threat of publicity and exposure, the pressure of relatives. The cutting down or degrading of the spouse: "He is impotent; he is a homosexual; he is a tax-cheat; he hoards pornography; he covets little girls." "She is a nymphomaniac; she neglects her children; she is frigid; she likes young studs."

Having generally considered the kinds of matrimonial clients lawyers deal with, and having discussed the general legal framework within which they work, let us reflect a moment upon the legitimate goals of the lawyer himself. Is he a mechanic who simply uses his skills to do his client's bidding, or should he have discretion to attempt to change or modify his client's desires? We think the latter.

Lawyers are under no obligation, and should have better sense than to make a client's personal vendetta their own. It is entirely reasonable and proper for a lawyer to attempt to dissuade an enraged husband from a course of conduct which is either legally or morally reprehensible. Instead of interfering (as many lawyers do) when wives, after due reflection, decide for themselves that they do not want what the law offers or what the lawyer can get but want considerably less, the lawyer should listen. Although we do not read about such wives, many exist, and their reasons should be respected. Lawyers frequently hear a woman say, "It is not his fault, I simply do not love him any more," or, "I found somebody else and do not think it is fair to ask him for a lot of money, although I think it is kind to hide the fact that there is somebody else from my husband." Or, "I have been dependent on that son-of-a-bitch for twenty years, and I am perfectly able to take care of myself, and that is what I want to do."

Lawyers are not paid to philosophize or to render moral judgments, and where the client is not posturing or engaging in momentary self-deception, it is the client's wishes, and not the lawyer's, which should prevail. The husband who says, "She has been a good wife and a good mother and I want to see to it that she gets the most, and not the least" is obviously to be respected as much as the one who entreats the lawyer to make sure that his wife gets as little as possible.

With the foregoing principles firmly in hand, we now contemplate what happens when lawyer meets client. In some ways the script is very similar for both husbands and wives, and in other respects the lawyer proceeds very differently, depending upon whether his client is the husband or the wife.

Regardless of sex, it is obviously important that the lawyer discover what his client's real desires are. Some clients go to lawyers simply for the purpose of being talked out of a divorce. Others go to complain about their mates and to unburden themselves. Some go to be assured by an authority-figure that it is all right to stay married; even though the husband gambles, the wife drinks, they both refrain from sex, or they do not much communicate any more. When assured that lots of couples live in such circumstances, the client skips happily home, greatly relieved to learn that others are just as miserable as he is, or to learn that marriage "happily ever after" is not the norm.

But where divorce has been decided upon, it then becomes essential to arm the lawyer. The personal history of the client and his other past marriages must be described in detail. Not only the shortcomings of the mate, but the transgressions of the client must be extracted.

It is also essential for the lawyer to know who wants the divorce most, his client or his adversary's. It is obvious that the lawyer whose client is most anxious for divorce is at a disadvantage. While there are really very few holdouts in matters matrimonial (i.e., clients who truly wish to stay married when they know their mates do not), every lawyer likes to begin each negotiation with, "Well, you know, my client really does not want to get out of this and I am not sure whether I can persuade him (or her) to change his (or her) mind." Translation for husband: "If you are in a hurry, the price is going to go up"; for the wife: "If you are in a hurry, you will have to take less."

The primary area of investigation is: Who has the dough? How is it come by? Where is it? Does the other spouse know about it? Where are the records, e.g., bank statements, canceled checks, savings books, insurance policies, wills, brokerage statements, securities, bonds, tax returns, etc.?

HUSBAND: They are in my office.
LAWYER: Thank God.

Or

WIFE: I don't know, I think they are at home.
LAWYER: Does your husband know that you are contemplating a divorce?
WIFE: He is seeing Mr. So-And-So just about now.
LAWYER (*ringing for his secretary*): Call a cab for Mrs. X.
(*To Wife*) Go home and get all the documents you can and bring them here.

Scene 2
Husband and wife in a mad footrace to reach the drawer or safe and return to their lawyers' offices with the documents. Unfortunate truth: The winner wins a lot.

It is the husband who most often has the greatest amount of financial information. He is better able, usually, to list his and his wife's assets and to establish in detail their respective incomes, expenditures, and debts. Every lawyer asks his client to make such a list as the basic raw material out of which applications for temporary alimony, and later for permanent alimony, are made by the wife and resisted by the husband.°

In order accurately to portray for the court, or for opposing counsel, the real financial picture of the parties, the lawyer must learn what kind of house or apartment the parties maintain, what kind of restaurants they eat in, how expensive are their wardrobes and gifts to each other, where they vacation, and where the money comes from.

HUSBAND: I don't have to worry about a thing. The yacht is owned by the corporation, the polo ponies belong to its subsidiary, our three-month trip to Europe was charged off to business, and I only receive twelve thousand a year as salary.
LAWYER: Now look, Mr. Executive, there are a few things you ought to know . . .
WIFE (*after enumerating her years of luxurious high living*

° In a third of the states husbands may seek alimony from their wives, but even in those states such applications are rare and are usually made to insulate the state against responsibility for caring for the husband.

and her absolute necessity for a maid, chauffeur, and gardener): But you should know that a few months ago my husband was disbarred and his father has disinherited him. Is that going to make a difference?

It all makes a difference, as does the fact that most couples do not lead lives of such extravagance and are barely able to make ends meet when living together. Indeed, many, if not most, live beyond their means in this credit-card economy; and when faced with the economic realities of divorce, discover painfully that their new lives will involve economic sacrifices beyond their abilities to comprehend in one, and sometimes in fifty visits to their lawyers' and accountants' offices.

Very significant to the lawyer is his own and his client's assessment of the extent to which the prospective divorce is going to be seriously contested, the amount of acrimony which has developed and which is likely to continue, and the client's ability to withstand the rigors of negotiation, and, if necessary, trial. The lawyer has to know how much time he has before his client's resolve dissipates or disappears. Resolute breast-beating in the lawyer's office, by either or both spouses, often disappears at joint conferences or when they go through the revolving door of the courthouse. Other clients seem to thrive and develop pride in their ability, with the help of their lawyers, to finally and equitably confront their mates. What the client says is sometimes of vital importance and sometimes worthless, and the lawyer frequently has to rely heavily upon his past experience and judgment.

Scene 1
LAWYER: Look, Mary, his threats aren't important. He can't take the children from you; he works for the home office of a corporation which is located in this state only and we have a court order directing him not to molest you.
WIFE: But he called me and said . . .
LAWYER: Mary, be strong. Don't talk to him.

Scene 2 (*Next day*)
WIFE: He says he's going to have you disbarred.
LAWYER: Mary, I'm not worried. Why are you? Why didn't you hang up when he called?
WIFE: Well, actually, I called him . . .

Or: Scene 1
HUSBAND: She said she can't live on what I'm giving her. She started to cry.
LAWYER: She cried when she told you she was living with another guy. She cried when she told you she didn't know what she was doing when she emptied the joint savings account. She cried when she confessed trying to get you fired. She . . .
HUSBAND: She's very mixed up.
LAWYER: She's mixed up but she has all the money, a boy friend, and a husband who's a sucker. When she tells the Judge you gave her extra money, he's going to assume you have it and you don't.
HUSBAND: Okay, okay.

Scene 2 (*Next day*)
HUSBAND: I told her this was going to be the last time.
LAWYER: Did she call you?
HUSBAND: Well, no, I called her to tell her that I couldn't afford . . .
LAWYER: You were lonely, weren't you, George?
HUSBAND: Well, she might change her mind . . .

The lawyer must of course know whether there is another man or another woman lurking in the background. This is of varying significance, depending upon whether one represents the husband or the wife and whether or not the other spouse is aware of the corespondent or corespondents. If the other mate is suspected of having a paramour, the question of hiring detectives must be considered (the art and cost of which we will discuss in a later chapter).

It is convenient, and sometimes crucial for the lawyer to know, if the client does, who will be representing the other side. Obviously if the lawyers know and respect each other, the job at hand is easier. It is curious, however, how repugnant it is to the wife to learn that her lawyer knows and does not hate the other lawyer. Aware of this, many wives' lawyers walk right past their friends representing the husband, wishing to avoid the wives' suspicion that the men are conspiring against them. Sometimes, knowing the name of the other lawyer simply means that meaningful negotiation and an amiable settlement is practically impossible. Some lawyers dote on their reputations as "hard guys" or simply as "obnoxious intransigents," with whom productive negotiations, short of the courthouse steps, are virtually impossible, except in bouts like this on the phone:

LAWYER X: Hello, Lawyer Toughguy? I am in the such-and-such matter. What's your client looking for?
LAWYER TOUGHGUY: As usual, the moon.
LAWYER X: When was the last time you got it?
LAWYER TOUGHGUY: *Click.*

In the interest of our readers, we have decided to go directly out on a limb and inform you that those of you who are attracted to Lawyer Toughguy should have your heads examined and deserve what you get—usually a lot of promises and a big bill.

Of course, the subject of fees should be brought up at an appropriate time. For a lawyer representing a husband, the best time is after the client has had impressed upon him the real necessity of learning the extent of his wealth and income. There is a natural reluctance on the part of husbands to make this disclosure to lawyers, who will in part base their fees upon the information. Nevertheless, full disclosure must be made, even though not only his lawyer, but also his wife, may benefit thereby.

We come now to the special considerations encountered by the lawyer when dealing with the wife. Is she being mistreated, is she being supported or starved out by the husband, is she in danger of physical abuse by the husband, does she suspect the husband of infidelity, and has she appointed herself her own detective? Has she a lover and is she still seeing him, is she denying her husband the right to see the children if the parties are living apart, is she poisoning the children's minds against the husband? Has she or does she intend to go on a spending spree, charging everything in sight (and a few baubles under the counter)? Is she being advised by her family and friends, and is she able to tell them to go to hell (nicely)? Does she need medical attention or psychiatric aid? (Nice evidence.) Is she planning to call the husband's employer, annoy his friends, and generally slander him in the community?

It's plain and simple, folks. The wife should indulge in none of the above activities without the prior knowledge and approval of her lawyer, and except for visiting the doctor and psychiatrist, such approval is rarely given.

> WIFE: He will never find out, we are very careful.
> LAWYER: That's what they all say.
> WIFE: He's screwing around, why can't I?
> LAWYER: You are asking for alimony, he is not.
> WIFE: I only did it when I found out he was.
> LAWYER: It doesn't make any difference.
> WIFE: That's not fair.
> LAWYER: Go live in another state if the law is unfair here.
> WIFE: What if I commit adultery in another state?
> LAWYER: Forget it.
> WIFE: Can I talk to him on the phone?
> LAWYER: Do you each have your own pay stations?
> WIFE: Really, now—
> LAWYER: If you have, okay.
> WIFE: Can I see him for lunch?
> LAWYER: Alone, or with somebody else?

And so on and so on. At this point the lawyer and the client negotiate. Sometimes the lawyer wins and the client agrees to stop the relationship altogether. More often than not, a compromise is reached where the adultery stops but communication with the paramour continues, and every private detective has a portfolio of photos to illustrate the many cases where the negotiation failed and the lawyer lost.

The answer to when and under what circumstances wives should engage in some of the more widely popularized and publicized vindictive behavior patterns, so often reported in the press and so abhorrent to the courts, depends in part upon the correlative behavior of the husband (which we will consider shortly), depends significantly upon whether a trial seems likely, and depends simply upon good taste and decorum. Courts cannot abide aggressive behavior by women and are unsympathetic, to say the least, to it.

But what the wife and her attorney will do, obviously depends upon the husband and his behavior during settlement negotiations and during litigation. If the husband fails to support the wife, closes normal accounts that have not been misused, physically abuses or threatens the wife, her family, friends, and employers, then her natural feelings of self-preservation and frustration create an ever-widening and ever more expensive conflagration.

So the parties and their advisers must decide whether they will take the high road or the low road in their quest for victory. Many husbands decide, knowing their wives, that starvation and agressive behavior cannot be withstood by the mate even temporarily, and many a wife has succumbed to her husband's harsh demands and terms of surrender simply to achieve an end to hostilities. The husband's gamble is that the wife will surrender quickly, before the case comes to court, or even before an application for temporary support or for a temporary order of protection may be ruled upon. Some browbeaten husbands and wives, after years or decades of timidity, are beaten before they start; convinced, in spite of their lawyers' attempts to reason otherwise, that the divorce will end, as the marriage has, with them as the poor, battered loser. So why endure all the pain?

But the gamble, particularly at the beginning, that the case will never go to court, and the parties' conduct will never be scrutinized by a judge, is a weighty one. And most cases, although not the most publicized ones, involve some attempt by the attorneys to restore order, pending trial or negotiation. They do so not only because of their professional objectivity and sense of fair play, but out of a justified fear of the court's wrath, should the respective clients' misconduct be brought out in court.

We mentioned earlier the special problems which must be attended to by the attorney representing the husband. If the spouse is vindictive, then charge accounts must be closed, although in large cities it sometimes seems that it is easier for the wife to open new accounts than it is for the husband to close old ones. If the wife is warping the children's minds, threatening employers, etc., then the husband too must harden his position and be more agressive in his own defense. If the wife is represented by Lawyer Toughguy, the husband's lawyer must act accordingly.

We are obviously portraying in this chapter what happens when the parties or their lawyers go too far. It presents the predictable results of irrational behavior too often triggered by the oppressive and cumbersome legal machinery that requires a winner and a loser. Where fault is demanded by the law, the parties often go too far in supplying it.

But we do not imply that every couple and its lawyers resort to smear or sink to the sordid tactics used by so many others. Some married people maintain their composure and dignity. They seek justice and not retribution, and accept their fate even when they are hardly elated by it. They give the court the minimum proof required for whatever the state's demands for "fault," and then divide honestly, and with just disclosure, the real assets of both or either, making provisions for the support of the wife and children, depending on the essential factors involved. What began in love can then end, at last, in friendship and trust. It happens; but alas, it does not happen often enough.

And what about the husband's girl friends?

HUSBAND: Can I see my girl friend?
LAWYER: I wish you would not.

HUSBAND: Why not? I want a divorce anyway.

LAWYER: Some courts will hold it against you and figure that if you have enough money to run around with other women, you have enough to support your wife.

HUSBAND: Does the law say that if I am guilty I have to pay more?

LAWYER: (*in most states*): No, that is not what the law says, but that is the way the judge acts.

HUSBAND: What if I get caught?

LAWYER: The judge will either envy you, sympathize with your wife, or think nothing of it. If you want to gamble, it is up to you.

The existence of a lover who the client, whether husband or wife, intends to marry immediately after the prospective divorce is of crucial importance to the tactics employed by the lawyer. If the wife has such a lover, it may be decidedly in her interest to try and arrange either an agreement or decree of divorce (if the state law permits) by which the husband makes a lump-sum settlement. Since alimony payments to the wife ordinarily terminate upon her remarriage, the imminence of such an event would obviously dispose her attorney to suggest—or better yet, to have the husband's lawyer suggest—such an arrangement. A great deal of the negotiation preceding a matrimonial settlement involves the allocation to be made between support for the wife and support for the children. Regular payments of such support to the wife are tax deductible to the husband, and includable by the wife in her tax returns. The husband normally prefers that as much as possible of the support given to the wife and children be allocable to the wife, not only because they are tax deductible but also because they terminate upon her remarriage.

The wife, however, would prefer to have the allocation favor the children. Where the husband does not know of the existence of the lover and believes, as many do, that the wife will never remarry and that he will be paying alimony for the rest of her life, the notion of a lump-sum settlement may sound very attractive.° Many a husband has made a lump-sum settlement upon the wife, only to find out to his horror that three days after the divorce she has taken as a new mate some pot-head rock-singer in a group pad, whom she is supporting with his money. But lump-sum settlements, to those who can afford them, sometimes are very attractive to the husband who wishes to know the limit of his liability to the wife, and who has a marked distaste for dealing with her in the future.

Here, too, many a husband has been surprised to learn that in some states, such as New York, where the wife improvidently dissipates the lump sum, she can still go to court and receive support for herself. And certainly no husband can discharge his obligations to the children by a lump-sum settlement where they are left penniless after the wife has squandered away not only her money but theirs too.

The tax consequences to husbands and wives of various kinds of settlements and court decrees, and indeed the very fact that payments have been made by the husband for the support of his wife and children prior to these agreements and decrees (usually not deductible by the husband for either wife or children), are of major importance to the clients. One husband may pay considerably more as alimony for the wife and children than another husband but have far more tax-free dollars available to himself. Clients are frequently horrified to find out how much more poorly they have done than they had thought after the I. R. S. probes into their arrangements. And some are correspondingly delighted to find that they have received windfalls not contemplated by their mates when the marriage was terminated.

With the designation of counsel for both sides, the real battle is under way. The lawyers meet, and the possibility of settle-

---

° The question of who pays the tax on such lump-sum settlements depends on a variety of complicated circumstances such as the period of time over which it is payable and whether such payments are unrestricted or contingent upon subsequent events.

ment is explored. It has been estimated that approximately 85 per cent of the divorces obtained in this country are arranged by agreement of the parties. To judge by the grounds for divorce that exist in the various states and upon which divorces are usually granted, one would conclude that we are a nation of adulterers, wife-beaters, alcoholics, and worse. But the reality is that since each state has its peculiar "grounds" for divorce, the case which is proven in court is simply one of form, by which the plaintiff (usually the wife) testifies without opposition to the defendant's conduct, thereby covering the formalities to the satisfaction of the uninterested justice presiding. Usually the financial arrangements have been made before, in terms of the separation agreement or stipulation that is incorporated into the decree of divorce.

Where there are few assets to be divided and where the husband's income is no secret (for example, he is employed regularly and has no other outside sources of income), the lawyers' task is considerably easier. The wife may end up with anywhere from 25 per cent to 50 per cent of the husband's income, depending upon the circumstances of the case, and particularly upon the duration of the marriage, the number and age of the children, the ability of the wife to work, etc. The lawyers' major goal in these uncomplicated cases is to lessen the clients' respective rancors, to show them on paper how little the other spouse is left with, and to demonstrate how costly and time-consuming litigation would be which might end up with approximately the same results—but minus the necessary legal and other court costs. But even where the case is uncomplicated from a financial standpoint, there remains the troublesome area where one party is "guilty" and the other wishes to take advantage of it. In many states, the court may not grant alimony to a wife (though it may grant support for children) who is the "guilty" party. The husband may maintain, and frequently does, that he does not care that the wife, who has brought up two lovely children, was seduced at a party on a single occasion while drinking four martinis, and that she is genuinely contrite.

OUTRAGED HUSBAND: I want to get rid of that slut.

LAWYER: "Tell me, have you never strayed?"

OUTRAGED HUSBAND: Only on business trips and at conventions, and that's different.

LAWYER: Why?

OUTRAGED HUSBAND: Whose side are you on?

LAWYER: Do you realize that it may cost you seventy-five-hundred dollars to prove your case, in nondeductible lawyers' fees and court costs? Do you realize that support for your wife is tax deductible, and that since she is gorgeous and only twenty-four she will probably remarry before you ever pay her that much in alimony?

OUTRAGED HUSBAND: Well, uh, I'll think about it.

Another Scene

WIFE: That son-of-a-bitch was screwing around with my best friend, while I was having the baby. I won't take any settlement, I want that bastard to be punished.

LAWYER: But he is willing to give you as much support as the court will award, and he is willing to give you the house, which is in his name, which the court in some states cannot award.

WIFE: I want that bastard crucified.

LAWYER: He is willing to take out an insurance policy naming you and the baby as irrevocable beneficiaries; the court cannot make him do that (in some states) either. And he is willing to give you ten thousand dollars in cash, and the court (in many states) cannot make him do that, either.

WIFE: You mean to say . . . while I was in the hospital having his child . . . and he and my best friend were . . .

Is this the way people behave? Have we portrayed the exceptional or caricatured Dagwood-Blondie, Jiggs-Maggie couples and how they would have ended their marriages? Unfortunately, no. It takes very little to edge once-sensible people into the "strategies" described.

When you observe the emotional setting in which divorce usually arises and the system by which it is disposed of, it's not hard to understand why matters get out of hand so badly. Faced with emotional and financial insecurity and forced to be "at war" after they have been trying to be a "team" for years or decades, men and women simply become overwhelmed. They each form a new team—themselves and their lawyers.

Obviously, many couples do keep their cool, able to exchange financial information and agree among themselves and their counsel on a fair settlement. They do so despite and not because of the system. They (and their lawyers) can put aside such notions as fault, guilt, and revenge, and are independent enough emotionally and strong enough physically to dissolve the past without conjuring up the demons of the future.

It is also true that some hurts are so heinous and some wrongs so vicious that emotion inevitably overcomes logic, and revenge seems a more legitimate goal than reason.

Even where we begin by saying we will be civilized men and women and will do nothing to hurt the children, we end by ignoring our promises when we disapprove of the tactics of our husbands or wives. Our nerves are so frayed and our feelings so fragile that it takes very little to nudge us into an ever-widening course of destruction and fury.

The responsibility of the lawyer and other marital advisers is to try to keep the client in emotional check and to direct his attention to the limited area of divorce that is the law's concern. Emotions cannot be shut off, but they can be deflected from becoming the base on which new lives are to be built.

This blurring of a legitimate desire for a fair settlement by an urgent need for revenge takes many shapes, and is almost always present. While the lawyer must be sympathetic, his major task is to achieve marital dissolution that will be fruitful long after the pain and anguish subside.

Most jurisdictions have procedures by which applications may be made for temporary alimony and temporary counsel fees. In New York, for example, the wife may proceed to the Supreme Court and make what is known as a "motion" for such relief, which consists of affidavits (sworn statements) by her, her witnesses, and her attorney, setting forth the reasons why she is unable to support herself or her children or to pay her counsel until the trial is reached six months to a year later. She may also proceed to the Family Court and petition for support. She may prefer the latter course when she requires support but does not want to give her husband a divorce or separation (where she knows he wants one), as motions for temporary alimony may only be made in cases in which divorce, separation, or annulment are sought. Or she may prefer the Family Court because a fairly immediate hearing is ordered there, and her husband's finances may be more realistically scrutinized during the course of a speedier trial, where his records as well as other financial records may be subpoenaed. There are many advantages and disadvantages to either procedure, and indeed many disadvantages to the very fact of giving a litigant a choice of courts in which to air his grievances.

But one way or another, wives who are not being supported and who are unable to support themselves, and wives or husbands who are being physically abused or whose children are, and those who are being locked out of their apartments and houses, may receive rather prompt remedial disposition by the court, even before trial.

Where the wife's application is made on affidavits, and even where prompt hearings are ordered, there is an unfortunate tendency on the part of husbands and their advisers to go for the "quick kill." The husband often maintains, untruthfully, that his wife is misbehaving in one way or another, that he is losing his job, or that his business has been ruined, that he is in debt, in ill health, etc. Here, again, this sort of husband engages in this kind of perjury, or gross exaggeration, because if he can successfully starve out his wife, or be directed to pay her an inadequate allowance pending trial, he feels that she will have no alternative but to submit to his demands before trial. Or he may do so because he or his advisers believe that by the time the trial arises he can bury the boodle so that the wife and her counsel will not be able to find it.

We mentioned before the nonexistent computer that would be

helpful in matrimonial proceedings. The shenanigans of a wife's exaggerations of her husband's income or a husband's "instant-poverty syndrome," are made possible not only by the militant inclinations of warring spouses but by the system itself.

Husbands and wives simply do not normally acquaint each other, in good times or bad, with the financial realities, and the law very often makes no provisions for this until it is too late; sometimes tragically too late to do either any good.

In some states, confrontations between wives and husbands prior to trial are regarded as so inflammatory that applicable court rules and decisions do not permit examinations before trial. In New York, the rules relating the pretrial discovery (the examination under oath of the parties, recorded by a court stenographer) are interpreted differently from county to county. For example, in Manhattan and the Bronx such examinations are forbidden except in very rare cases, while in Nassau County, Brooklyn, and Westchester they are allowed rather freely.

Where the lawyers have to wait until trial to learn the true state of the finances of their adversary's client, the resulting confusion frequently makes the trial a charade. First the wife is put on the stand, then her witnesses, and then the husband. Very often the husband's attorney wheels into court cartons, stacked on a dolly, of financial records which he and his advisers have been poring over, culling, and editing for months. The judge will allow the wife's lawyer minutes, hours, or perhaps overnight, to examine all of these records in order to examine the husband concerning his bank accounts, savings accounts, stock transactions, business affairs, and manipulations over a period of years. In these instances even the husband's lawyer finds himself faced for the first time with often innovative explanations of what happened to all the money the wife inherited from her Uncle Harry and how, pending trial, her little antique business has suddenly started to show tremendous losses.

Where examinations before trial are permitted, they are extremely helpful; but as they are usually held out of the presence of the court, counsels' objections and cries of "irrelevant" and protestations that the information being sought is privileged or not yet available or in the hands of third parties (such as relatives, employers, partners, business associates, etc.) are endless. And even after the examination is concluded, between then and the trial, how often the parties' fortunes change—and rarely for the better (to hear them tell it)!

In a recent case in New York, after what husband and wife later testified had been twenty-five years of marital bliss, the husband awoke on his fiftieth birthday and decided that since he and his wife were no longer having sexual relations, he would leave her. The next day, he brought his wife a cup of coffee, told her he was leaving, and left. At that time, so far as his wife knew and so far as the financial statements he had left behind indicated, his business was flourishing, he owned various securities and a Mercedes-Benz, and he was well able to continue supporting his wife. He refused to do so, however, and the wife went to Family Court claiming nonsupport.

In Family Court the husband claimed that his wife had refused to have sexual relations with him for a period of over ten years, and the wife conceded that although they had not had sexual relations for over five years, it was because the husband was indifferent, and not she. She further testified that her husband had told her that he had found another woman.

After the first hearing, the court, interestingly enough, held that it believed the husband's testimony, but that the wife's refusal to have sexual relations was not deliberate but was caused by a "psychic block" which she had developed against sex. In short, the situation was no different than had she developed a physical ailment, and the husband was not justified in abandoning his wife. The court therefore directed a hearing on the parties' finances.

True to script, hubby and his lawyer announced that the husband's business and financial affairs were in chaos. The husband denied having a paramour and, sure enough, his latest tax returns showed that his income had declined from over $60,000 to less than $25,000, and a special audit done by the husband's accountants indicated that the picture was worsening.

In the meantime, the wife's counsel had been tipped off to some very interesting facts. The husband was moving his business to a southern state and was filtering large amounts of his corporation's money to the new business and to another business in that state. Moreover, he really did have a girl friend and she was residing with him at a posh address; and, sure enough, the lady turned out to be "the designer" for the husband's business.

The wife's lawyer promptly subpoenaed hubby's business accounts and checkbooks, and he subpoenaed the designer and found her bank accounts. Alas, while the husband's fortunes were on the decline and his business facing ruin, his designer was being given raise after raise. Beyond that, his designer (a young lady, twenty-two years his junior) had opened up a savings account in which her aging lover was named as beneficiary. The husband maintained that even though the lady was served with process outside of his apartment and had given his address when she opened the account, she was really only a friend and wanted to use his address as her mailing address. At first, the husband was asked:

(Mr. Sheresky) Q: Did you know that the name of that account is "Miss Jane Designer, in trust for Richard Executive?"
A: No, sir.
Q: And the first time you heard of that is today?
A: Yes, sir.

When confronted with the account, hubby then remembered it and "recalled" its details.

Q: In or about April of 1969, when the account Jane Designer in trust for Richard Executive was established, was there any conversation between you and Miss Designer?
A: Yes.
Q: Where was that conversation?
A: It was in New York City. I don't recall where.

Q: Who was present at it?

A: She was and I was.

Q: Do you remember whether it was at your place of business?

A: It might have been.

Q: Tell the court please what the substance of the conversation was, to the best of your recollection.

A: Well, as I recall it, Jane Designer told me that she was going to open this bank account and she wanted to put it in trust for me to manage her money for the welfare of her family, and especially her mother, in case anything happened to her. She was not leaving the money to me, and I certainly didn't need it, and she told me of her relationship with her mother. She trusted me implicitly that I would be able to handle it because her mother couldn't. This was simply a question, I presume, of being like a kind of executor or something like that, without making a will.

Q: And what did she tell you that she wanted you to do in the event that she passed away and the money then was left to you?

A: I should make sure that her mother wouldn't be able to spend it all and get rid of it, but it should be used to be apportioned out to the family as they needed it.

Q: How old is Miss Designer?

A: She's twenty-eight.

Q: Did you, in words or in substance, suggest to her that since you were somewhat older than she, she might perhaps pick a younger executor?

A: Yes; I mean I did suggest that to her, and the only thing is I don't know whether she was acquainted with the statistics about it or anything like that, but the point is that while I lived, she wanted it entrusted to me. If I died, then I guess she would entrust it to someone else.

Q: Did she at that time tell you that she had already had an account that was in trust for her mother?

A: I don't recall. Yes, I knew of the account and I knew that it was small, and she kept it very small too.

MR. SHERESKY: At this time, if Your Honor please, I will offer a transcript of the account of Jane Designer in trust for Richard Executive, account number —— in evidence.

Mr. Executive's Counsel: I have no objection, Your Honor.

Not only did Miss Designer have an account in trust for Mr. Executive, but it also turned out that he maintained an account in trust for Miss Designer. Whereupon he was asked:

Q: You have a son, do you not?
A: Yes, I do.
Q: How old is he?
A: Approximately twenty-four, twenty-four-and-a-half.
Q: Do you have any bank accounts in trust for him?
A: No, I do not.
Q: You have a mother, do you?
A: Yes, I do.
Q: Do you have any bank accounts in trust for her?
A: No, I do not.
Q: Do you have any bank accounts in trust for anybody else other than Jane Designer?
A: No, I do not.

It next turned out that during the summer of the same year in which Mr. Executive claimed to have been experiencing his worst financial disaster in years, he was able to vacation in France. He was asked:

Q: When you went to France, were you joined by Miss Designer?
A: Yes.
Q: Where did you stay?
A: You mean the itinerary?
Q: Yes, I do.
A: We went to Paris, and then traveled down to Cannes.
Q: And when you were in Paris, do you recall the hotel you stayed at?
A: No, I really don't. I don't remember the name.
Q: How long were you in Paris?
A: For three days, I believe.

Q: Do you remember where it was?

A: You mean the section of Paris?

Q: Yes.

A: I know it was near the Tuileries, but I just don't remember the name of the hotel.

Q: Was it the George V?

THE COURT: I really don't believe that a three-day-stay at any hotel would be very significant for a person's income, Mr. Sheresky, assuming he isn't alleging to be a complete pauper.

MR. SHERESKY: Well, it gets to be pretty expensive. He went other places.

Q: Where else besides Paris did you go?

A: We went down, as I said, from Paris down to Cannes.

Q: And do you remember where you stayed when you were in Cannes?

A: I don't recall the name of the hotel. I have a picture of it before my eyes, but I honestly cannot remember the name of it.

Q: How long were you at that hotel?

A: I think about five days.

Q: And other than Paris and Cannes, did you go anywhere else?

A: On the way down, a few one-night stops at some small hostelries on the road.

* * *

Q: Now when you went to Europe, whose funds did you use?

A: I used—when I went to Europe, I used my funds.

Q: Out of your checkbook?

A: I think some was out of my savings account. I don't recall whether it was a checkbook or a savings account. It might have been one or the other, or both.

Q: Did you fly?

A: Yes.

Q: How did you pay for the air fare?

A: If I recall, I think I paid for it through the AAA. I think I made the reservation through them, but I don't find any canceled check there, so I just at the moment cannot recall how I paid them.

Q: How did you pay for the hotels?

A: I don't recall either.

Q: What did the trip cost, do you remember?

A: I think the trip cost me about $750.

Q: Your fares for you and Miss Designer and the hotels cost $750.

A: I didn't pay for Miss Designer.

Q: Miss Designer paid for herself?

A: That's right.

Q: Did you stay together when you were on your trip?

MR. EXECUTIVE's COUNSEL: Objection. It certainly does not go to the question of finances. He's already testified she paid for herself and he paid for himself.

THE COURT: Well, I assume—I am hesitant to verbalize your contention. I think it is obvious. Your objection is overruled.

Q: Did you stay together?

A: Yes, we stayed together.

Q: And when it came time to pay for the hotel bill, you asked her for her half?

A: It just doesn't work like that, Mr. Sheresky. You don't—

Q: She offered it herself?

MR. EXECUTIVE's COUNSEL: Objection. You have asked a question, let him answer it.

THE COURT: I don't notice any substantial withdrawal on this account, Mr. Sheresky.

MR. SHERESKY: I know there isn't, Your Honor.

Q: She paid for her half of the hotel bills?

A: Yes, for all the expenses.

Q: She paid for her air fare?

A: That's correct.

Q: Did you rent a car?

A: Yes.

Q: She paid for half of it?

A: Yes.

Q: When you went and bought gas, who paid for that?

A: You're asking me who physically paid for it? I physically paid for it.

Q: Then she returned the money to you?

A: It isn't done every half-hour or half-day.

∗ ∗ ∗

Q: She gave you money. Did she give it to you by check or cash?

A: I really don't remember. It may have been cash, but I really don't remember.

Q: Did she give it to you before you took off in the airplane or after you got to Europe?

MR. EXECUTIVE'S COUNSEL: I am going to object, Your Honor. We have already admitted Mr. Executive booked a trip with Miss Designer and he gave the approximate amount of the cost, and I think at this point it just becomes a matter of badgering. We are not eliciting facts, just arguing with the witness.

THE COURT: It seems to me clear from the evidence that's already been given that there is some sort of commingling of funds of Mr. Executive and Miss Designer, and it seems to me that all of this further testimony along this line would show would be to that effect.

MR. SHERESKY: It might also show—

MR. EXECUTIVE'S COUNSEL: That there is a commingling of funds?

° ° °

Q: As I understand the arrangement between you and Miss Designer, it was that you were going to divide the expenses equally?

MR. EXECUTIVE'S COUNSEL: Objection; he didn't say they were going to divide the expenses equally.

THE COURT: That they were going to divide the expenses?

Q: Did you decide whether it was going to be equal or unequal?

A: It's hard for me to recall if we made a pact on it and agreed to split every penny down the middle. It's the kind of situation where each of us would pay our share, and I would say generally speaking that there would be a division of expenses there.

Q: And did there sometime at the end of this journey get to be a reckoning between you and Miss Designer as to who owed who money?

A: Yes.

Q: Where did that take place?

A: I don't recall. In New York.

Q: And who did it end up owing money, you or her?

A: I really don't recall.

When the husband was questioned about the flight of money from his business (we call it the XYZ Corporation here) in New York to the Southern state (let's call it Alabama), the testimony went as follows:

Q: Did you ever hear of XYZ of Alabama?

A: Oh, yes.

Q: What is that?

A: Well, that's a corporation that is owned by YXA of New York. I don't own any of it.

Q: When was that set up?

A: That was set up about four or five months ago—no, less, excuse me. It may have been three months ago.

Q: Is that a small company too?

A: Yes.

Q: And did XYZ Company put any money into this small Alabama corporation?

A: Perhaps $40,000 has been sent down there.

Q: Would $85,000 be closer to it?

A: Not that I'm aware of, no sir.

After a colloquy between court and counsel, the court directed the husband to call his bookkeeper and inform the court promptly what the correct figure was, and to produce the corporate checkbook. After an appropriate recess, the husband's counsel stipulated "that the figure of $80,000, as suggested by Mr. Sheresky, is correct."

Later on, when attempting to account for a $7000 "loan" made to the husband by Miss Designer from the trust account, the husband said he needed it and she agreed to lend it to him, although the terms of the loan were not agreed upon. The wife's lawyer pointed out to the husband that almost at the same time that he had borrowed $7000 from his designer, he was able to borrow $125,000 from his bank on his signature alone, and the husband had no ready explanation as to why he did not borrow $132,000 from the bank without troubling his "employee."

All examples given above, and dozens of other cases from every lawyer's file, illustrate the interminable and frustrating chase for assets and income, and the length to which some clients go to hide their existence. Under the present system, thousands of cases are unjustly decided because one client or the other simply has not been lucky enough or skillful enough or had sufficient money or time to spend unearthing the buried loot.

So it turns out that agreements are reached and awards of alimony made on the basis of patently misrepresented facts. It is often possible, if the spouse who has been lied to ultimately uncovers the truth, to set aside or modify agreements or decrees, or those parts of them relating to finances. But too often this procedure is lengthy, costly, or impossible because the treasure is buried too deep.

When the clients and their lawyers really put their minds to it, materimonial maneuvering and litigation can go on forever. Judge Louis Heller, in New York's Supreme Court, Kings County, when faced with such a situation eloquently and pungently described "The Thirty Years' War" between the combatants and dealt with it in his inimitable way. He said, in part:

When I asked the clerk to send the Sloan file to my chambers, a court officer wheeled in a furniture dolly on which was piled a tall bundle of heavy, overflowing files which document the Thirty Years' War between these embittered and embattled adversaries. Thus unfolded the sad saga of the spiteful Sloans.

To recount the multitudinous court skirmishes, motions to modify, . . . appeals, et cetera, which have occupied the court, the parties, and a succession of attorneys through the years would not be particularly rewarding, but a brief background of the parties' standard of living is in order.

During the years that the Sloans lived together, the defendant, then a small-to-middling manufacturer of ladies' clothes, provided his family, consisting of plaintiff-wife, defendant, and a daughter (now thirty-six years old and self-supporting, who shares an apartment with her mother) in rather elegant style, residing in a fashionable apartment, with a maid, governess for the daughter, winter vacations in Florida and Havana, summer vacations at seashore and mountain resorts. They lived the good life until the defendant suffered severe business reverses just prior to the marital breakup.

Since the parties' separation, the defendant, after a series of business vicissitudes, prospered to the extent that he became nationally known as an entrepreneur of high-fashion ladies' sportswear. Contemporaneous with this success was an intimately personal and business association with a highly creative lady who is also nationally renowned as a designer. Throughout the numberless and interminable legal melees between the parties, the defendant has stoutly and modestly contended that the success of the Robert Sloan line of ladies' sportswear is due to the genius of his designer-paramour, and that his own biggest contribution to the enterprise was lending his name to the line. He has stuck to that line through the years.

Be that as it may, there is no gainsaying the fact that Robert Sloan and his designing lady make beautiful music together, as well as beautiful clothes. They maintain a Park Avenue apartment and a condominium villa in a luxurious resort area in Southern California, the latter purchased for the pampered pair by Robert Sloan Sportswear, Inc., in November, 1967. The corporation also paid and pays for all his traveling and entertaining expenses, and maintained charge accounts for his and his designer's benefit at Bergdorf Goodman, Henri Bendel, and other posh shops, not to mention credit cards with the Diners' Club and American Express. Defendant and his paramour traveled sumptuously and extensively, both throughout this country and abroad, and entertained and lived in a lavish manner consistent with the enormous success of their enterprise. They are still living exceedingly high on the hog.

In contrast, plaintiff and their daughter live in a small apartment on West Eighty-sixth Street in Manhattan, where they have lived since the plaintiff obtained her separation decree in 1944. The building, once fashionable, has deteriorated badly. The apartment house is rent controlled, unattended, and poorly maintained; tenants have been mugged in the lobby and elevator. The surrounding neighborhood has become a slum. Because of her limited funds, Mrs. Sloan has not refurnished or redecorated her apartment in many years.

Mrs. Sloan's precarious financial position was severely jeopardized when defendant unilaterally reduced his support payments to $50 per week in July, 1969, although his cross-motion to reduce plaintiff's support payments was still pending. Defendant offered his modest income and limited assets as the reason for this reduction. I may add at this juncture, that defendant's cross-motion to reduce alimony, which under the circumstances could only be described as ludicrous, was withdrawn at the conclusion of the instant hearing.

While it is true that when a husband and wife are separated the wife does not become a full partner to the husband's subsequent increased income and resources, the manner in which the parties lived prior to the separation and the defendant's present financial capacity are material considerations in determining what is a proper provision for plaintiff's support. The husband's capital in comparatively liquid form, his investments, portfolio, and other assets are considered. In determining the ability of defendant to adequately support his separated wife, the court is not controlled by his net income as reported in his income-tax returns, particularly, where, as in the instant case, the self-serving income of the husband is manipulated by the corporations controlled by himself and his partner.

The machinations of defendant in concealing his holding have frustrated plaintiff's previous attorneys through the years. However, the herculean efforts of her present attorneys have borne fruit. Despite every conceivable subterfuge, roadblocks, dilatory tactic, and ulcer-cultivating ploy utilized by defendant to impede discovery and inspection of his brokerage, bank, and corporate records, plaintiff's present attorneys' painstaking spadework lead to the uncovering of defendant's assets to the extent that a fair estimate of the value of his holdings at the present time, giving due consideration to the erratic gyrations of the stock market these past weeks, is between $700,000 and $800,000.

In view of the foregoing and upon all the evidence before me, including the proof of plaintiff's alleged necessary expenses, I will fix alimony for her support in the sum of $300 per week.

At the conclusion of the hearing on May 7, 1970, defendant was ordered to post a bond to insure the payment of alimony and necessary legal and accounting expenses in the sum of $150,000. To date he has not done so. It appears that he has systematically divested himself of, and transferred most of his assets to his paramour. It further appears that defendant and his paramour have gradually phased out their business operation in New York and have almost completed a clandestine move to the State of California. Plaintiff is granted leave to apply for additional counsel and accountant's fees if defendant's action make it necessary to engage counsel in California.

Defendant is put on notice that he will not be permitted to thumb his nose at the court with impunity. Trifling with the court's directives will be an expensive proposition.

In settlement negotiations the lawyers plod on, trying to give and to get information adequate for a realistic estimate of the results they can achieve for their clients. The same process happens when negotiations fail and the case proceeds toward trial. Hopefully, by asking enough questions, by doing enough independent investigation, and by using their experience, they can reach a point where the legitimate perimeters of fairness become apparent. Then comes the process of explaining to the client why his or her reasonable expectations are met or are about to be met. Where this occurs, productive agreements can be written or amicably arranged divorces can proceed to trial.

Then the court, at the request of both attorneys, usually decrees what has theretofore been agreed to by the parties. Of course, finances are not the only consideration. Custody and visitation rights concerning the children, the division of household property, who gets the dog, and who gets the football tickets, whether and where the children go to camp, private schools, and colleges, etc., must be agreed upon, and are considered later when we deal with separation agreements.

By now it should be apparent to the reader that the adversary system of justice breaks down far too often in resolving matrimonial conflict. It is equally true that negotiations and amicable divorces are concluded partially in the dark, and that agreements are often reached after insufficient exploration and sober reflection. Too much in our system is dependent upon trick and artifice, upon the skills of the lawyers, upon the agressiveness or passivity of the client, and upon the harshness or leniency of the laws of a particular state and how they are used or misused. The system is bad enough when there are no children involved. It is often catastrophic when they are. Concepts of blame or guilt, accusation and counteraccusation should have no place in the dissolution of most relationships where the parties want out, whatever their reasons.

It is obvious that marital combatants and their lawyers must be disarmed. To us, the easiest way would be to get rid of the necessity of proving fault, to recognize dead marriages, and to create a system whereby the parties are obliged, under heavy financial—and perhaps even criminal—penalties, to truthfully submit to searching examinations concerning their finances, perhaps before court referees with experience in accounting.

Too many harsh decisions by courts applying rigid and punitive rules have shown that marriages cannot be equitably terminated by fitting complicated facts into inflexible statutes. Matrimonial legislation that condemns all adultery or all abandonment, or which imposes economic sanctions against other behavior, regardless of the cause, simply does not work. So long as our laws require the litigants to be lily-white, and so long as they are indifferent to the complex reasons for our behavior in marriage, and so long as they prevent judges from inquiring into the complete factual background against which matrimonial transgressions occur, perjury will abound; and courts will continue to hear evidence designed to please the legislators but which bears little resemblance to the real reasons why the marriage broke down. Without this real evidence, determination of how much support wives and children should receive is made impossible.

Hard-and-fast rules by which property and income are divided according to immutable concepts of "legal title" must give way to flexible standards that may be applied to the infinite variety of factual circumstances leading to divorces. Separation and divorce decrees should be in accordance with what is fair and just in a particular marriage. If the court is given discretion to do what is right, the parties are far more apt to reach a settlement than when they carry the unnecessary armament of "fault" concepts, and assumptions of matrimonial "defenses" which only obfuscate the search for equity in dissolving marriages.

Matrimonial reform—such as the abolition of traditional concepts of fault, the repeal or modification of divorce laws that discriminate against husbands or wives because of sex, and legislation which permits courts, in their discretion, to award alimony and property according to what is fair with respect to each individual marriage, considering its entire history—is more and more becoming a reality.

It is urgently needed and in time it will be a reality in every state.

CHAPTER 7

Changing Your Mind

WIFE: I am not sure whether I want this or not, but I need a change.
HUSBAND: For Christ's sake, Cynthia, you aren't trying on a new dress, you know. Once we get through with the God-damned lawyers, and tell the children, things will never be the same.

Or

MOTHER: You are ruining your life. Get out while you are still young, dear. If you want, you can always change your mind. He'll come back to you.
WIFE: I suppose you are right. He has never looked at another woman in the ten years we've been married.

Or

WIFE: I like you, Henry, but I just don't love you any more.
HUSBAND: I still love you, but I am starting not to like you.
WIFE: Just a trial separation. We won't even tell the children. We'll tell them you have to live somewhere else because of business.

We have just described an indecisive group, to say the least. It is one thing to reflect seriously upon divorce, to analyze its advantages and disadvantages, to seek qualified help in deter-mining whether one should go ahead with it, to threaten the wife with it ("to keep her in line") or the husband with it ("to make him pay more attention," of course), but it is quite another to actually take the plunge. Fees of psychiatrists, marriage counselors, and lawyers aside, the extent to which spouses can vacillate once the "decision" to divorce is reached can range from imperceptible to drastic.

WIFE (*on the phone*): Henry, I am not so sure about this now. Can't we go out Saturday night, like we used to?
HUSBAND (*impatiently waiting to return to the teen-ager he never dreamed would find him attractive*): Well, I don't know if that's such a good idea. I think you were quite right, and now that we are apart we ought to make very certain that we know what we want to do. How about lunch on Wednesday —and could you bring me my suitcase? I'm going away next weekend on a business trip.

Once parties separate, predictable patterns occur. At first loneliness sets in, which is particularly painful for those who are used to family life even if the domestic routine involved only bickering and neglect. The familiar sights and sounds are gone, and the urge is to do something, or find something to replace them. Again husbands find it far easier "to get back into circulation." Their memory of what "circulation" means is very pleasantly aroused. Conservative, dour, button-down types may acquire new hair-do's, new wardrobes, and become middle-aged hippies. The vision of other women with fewer demands (they think) replaces the fear that loneliness is the aftermath of divorce.

Some wives may also find that their new freedom generates a new independence. If they are lucky enough to attract men, their deep fears of the aging process may then recede.

But in a male-dominated society, the hopes and expectations of the "trial divorcée" are usually not fulfilled. Lone women, particularly those with children, are drugs on the American youth market.

The decision to divorce should in any case not be a game-playing process. Its dangers are too numerous, and usually irrevocable. Some birds return to their cages, but most do not.

During the divorce process many married people really want to change their minds, but are simply too proud to do so. They are advised, "Are you kidding? Can a zebra change his stripes? He [or she] is still the same So-And-So you married." Very often true, but a glimpse of the single world may convince the more mature that the sea of matrimony may be calmer and less forbidding than other waters.

> LAWYER TOUGHGUY: Go back now, when we've got the goods on him?
> WIFE: But he has been calling me, and I really miss him.
> LAWYER TOUGHGUY: The stuff we've got on him is too good to throw away.
> WIFE: Do I get my fee back?
> LAWYER TOUGHGUY: That's not my policy.

When it comes to a client changing his or her mind, it is a good general rule that lawyers should mind their own business. This doesn't mean that they shouldn't try to determine whether the client is experiencing a temporary or a wholly irrational change of mind. But the client who genuinely wants to return to a marriage should not be dissuaded from doing so, however dubious this solution may appear to the lawyer. And any lawyer who attempts such dissuasion is a meddler or a damned fool.

In many states, to be sure, there is a defense of condonation, by which the law maintains that if a party truly forgives another, such forgiveness bars future complaints about past misdeeds, which are knowingly forgiven.° It must be unhappily reported that there have been husbands and wives who have returned to the marital abode, once their transgressions have been discovered, for the sole purpose of having them condoned. These cynical opportunists are rare, however, and most (but not all) courts hold that such condonation is an effective bar to subsequent complaints only if the offenses which have been con-

---

° "Parties to a cause of divorce may not litigate by day and copulate by night . . ." (*Holt* v. *Holt*, 77 F 2d 538, 540).

doned are not again repeated and have been fully disclosed. A wife who resumes living with the husband who has admitted having a "one-night stand" on a business trip is not considered to have condoned his ten-year affair with his secretary, about which she never knew, or the new affair upon which he is about to embark.

CHAPTER 8

Separation Agreements

Separation agreements are contracts containing the terms and conditions under which the parties agree to live separate and apart. As the laws of separation and divorce vary from state to state, so too do they differ concerning the crucial questions of what is and what is not permissible to insert in such agreements. One state considers all such agreements invalid unless they are incorporated into (i.e., made a part of) a divorce decree, or unless they are signed after the marriage is terminated. And in at least one state, such an agreement is valid only where legal grounds exist for separation or divorce. Usually, however, the necessity for guilt is not required.

Many courts have said that agreements of separation are not valid unless the parties are living apart, although the courts interpret this requirement differently. In New York, for example, separating spouses frequently reside together until they are either divorced or separated by the court, or until after an agreement is signed. They are encouraged to do so by the courts. Physical separation, however, must "immediately" follow the execution of the agreement, although courts differ on what is the meaning of "immediately."

Agreements of separation which are regarded as inducements to a subsequent divorce are frequently, as in New York, held to be against public policy favoring marriage, although the decisions and the applicable statutes are often hard to reconcile as to what constitutes an inducement. Obviously increasing the wife's boodle, if she gets a divorce, would be considered to be such an inducement. But in New York, at least, a provision stating that the agreement will terminate if the parties are still married within x number of months or years would be upheld.

Agreements between husbands and wives will be scrutinized to make sure that they are not the products of fraud, coercion, or overreaching. Agreements prepared by one attorney acting for both parties will more likely be set aside as unfair or oppressive than agreements in which the parties are represented by different attorneys—invariably the desired case.

Financial misrepresentations by either party should not be made lightly, since they may result either in the total invalidity of the agreement or in retention of those terms of the agreement most beneficial to the deceived spouse.

More often, however, a spouse is required to choose whether to stand on the agreement or repudiate it.

Separation agreements must be made between people who are validly married, and the existence of another spouse at the time the agreement is signed will make it invalid. The parties, under applicable state laws, must be old enough to contract and of sufficient mental capacity to know what they are doing.

State law may prohibit the insertion of other provisions repugnant to the policy of the state. In New York, for example, provisions for relieving a husband of the obligation to support the wife or of permitting him, at his discretion, to determine the amount of support, or providing patently inadequate provision for support will all be stricken, although the agreement itself may still stand. Lump-sum settlements are also regarded with disfavor in some states, such as New York, and an agreement providing for such payments may be set aside where the proceeds of the settlement, regardless of how generous, have been exhausted by the wife and she is likely to become a public charge.

Where the wife claims that the provision for her was inadequate, the subsequent affluence of the husband has been often said to be irrelevant as to whether the agreement should stand, but many inroads have been made in this area. In the first place, children are not parties to the agreement and applications may frequently be made on their behalf to increase the support allocable to them, and in New York and elsewhere courts have concluded by statute or by decision that under varying theories they are empowered to grant relief to an impoverished wife whose husband has substantially increased his earning power or assets. They do so by setting the agreement aside as being inadequate, or again, upon the ground that the wife may become a public charge unless the court intervenes. Where the agreement has been incorporated into a subsequent decree of divorce or separation, courts frequently say that while the agreement stands, they have either the statutory (as in New York) or inherent authority to modify their own decrees and to change the provisions for support of wife and/or children, in the interests of justice and in the light of a substantial change of circumstances of the parties, or upon the theory that the state is a party to the contract and its courts have the power to do what is just. The same statutes, decisions, and judicial reasoning may be applied where the husband's subsequent financial circumstances are drastically reduced and he simply cannot afford to abide by the original agreement. Many states provide relief for such a husband (again, particularly where the terms of the agreement have been incorporated into a decree of separation or divorce). Many courts simply fail to uphold the wife's attempts to enforce the agreement—as, for example, where the wife seeks to hold the husband in contempt or to jail him for nonpayment. The law in this important field is extremely murky and rapidly changing. Our courts are struggling to reconcile constitutional concepts of freedom of contract with varying legitimate policies regarding the changing needs of husbands, wives, and their children in the light of subsequent events beyond their power of contemplation.

We will consider later another concept of the upward or

downward modification of divorce and separation decrees and agreements that have been incorporated into them and which, normally, by the express terms of the agreement, "survive" (roughly, exist independently of) such decrees. But we emphasize that once an agreement is signed, a substantial change in circumstances must be demonstrated before a spouse can be relieved of its provisions. And often—very often—no relief or too little relief is available. Constitutional concepts of freedom of contract, and feelings that there should be an end to marital warfare, greatly inhibit the power and desire of legislators and courts to interfere with agreements reached by adults, each represented by independent counsel. Where relief is available, the change of circumstances must be drastic and must go beyond mere demonstration of the increasing ages and requirements of children, the fact that there is inflation and the dollar worth less, and other subsequent situations which should have been contemplated by the parties at the time they entered their agreement.

The question frequently raised by women is whether, after the signing of a separation agreement, they may proceed to conduct themselves normally (translation: can they screw around?). Consult your local lawyer; the question is a very tricky one. In New York she is free to do so—if the agreement is properly drafted.

A provision in a separation agreement providing for the wife's support (but not the children's) terminates upon her remarriage unless otherwise stated. Thus not only social but hard economic realities can explain why the divorced wife may live with a man and sometimes even bear his children, without actually marrying him. Some agreements contain a *dum casta* ("while chaste") provision which specifies that "remarriage" shall include the continuous living of the wife with another man. The validity of such a provision is questionable. The fact that the wife is engaging in such conduct, however, may well bear upon questions of custody.

In some states the very existence of separation agreements is crucial in providing a "no-fault" ground for subsequent divorce.

In New York, and in many other states, it is a ground for divorce that the parties have lived separate and apart pursuant to an agreement or decree for periods of time specified in the governing statute. Some states, of course, recognize this no-fault ground where the parties have been consentually living apart, regardless of the existence of an agreement or divorce.

It would be impossible to explain each of the provisions that go into separation agreements, and why and when they are put there. It should be obvious, however, that those agreements may last a lifetime, or beyond. They should be as complete as possible, as well drafted as possible, and as reasonable as possible.

> HUSBAND: Damn it, Mr. X, I can't sleep, I can't work, my girl friend says that if I don't get out of my marriage now we are through. I'll sign anything.
> LAWYER: Look at the facts and figures. You'll never be able to live up to this agreement.
> HUSBAND: You'll see—my wife will realize that I can't live up to it and will change it.
> LAWYER (*reaching into the drawer for a Tums*): You're making a mistake."

Or

> WIFE: He loves his children. He's only giving them ten dollars a week, to hurt me. He'll change his mind. I want to sign this damn thing and get it over with.
> LAWYER (*reaching into the drawer for a Tums*): What if he has children by a new wife?
> WIFE: May I have one of those Tums?

Properly drafted agreements provide, among other things, for the following:

(a) The names and addresses of the parties and their children; the intention to make a complete and final agreement; the admission by both parties that they have had ample opportunity to determine, independently, each other's financial resources and their respective needs and the needs of the children; the fact that the agreement is intended to cover the division of all property held by them individually, jointly, or in trust for others; and any other relevant recitals, depending upon the facts of the case.

(b) The agreement should provide that the parties shall be free to live independent of each other and to pursue separate activities.

(c) It should describe in detail the personal property owned by the parties, its location, and how it is to be allocated. Very often this provision should be negotiated last because of the frequent invective triggered off when the parties quibble over trivia.

> HUSBAND: You get the kids, you get the house, you get the maid, you get the dogs, you get the Renoirs, you get $2000 a week pocket money. Damn it, I want Junior's bronzed shoes.
> WIFE: You bastard, you weren't even around when the kid was born.
> LAWYER X: Would you like a Tums?
> LAWYER Y: I've had four already.

Frequently the parties themselves should be made to resolve these problems, which sometimes take longer to accomplish than all of the other terms of the agreement.

(d) The question of who is to own or occupy real property: Who is to own, continue to lease, or to occupy what; whether the wife is to continue living in the apartment or the house, and for how long and under what circumstances; what happens to deposits on leases on apartments, or the proceeds of the sale of the house when the wife no longer lives there; what happens if the rental of the apartment or mortgage payments and interest rates increase; who pays the moving expenses when the wife moves?

There are a variety of tax consequences created by the disposition in separation agreements of real and personal property, and lawyers and clients should familiarize themselves with them before the agreement is signed. Tax problems, of course, pervade the entire negotiation and execution of separation agreements, and at times are crucially important in determining whether the agreement is fair and equitable.

(e) Alimony for the wife and support for the children: ° How much does the wife get and how much is allocated to the children; when does the wife's alimony cease and under what circumstances is it to be reduced; does she get less when the children are away at camp or college or after they are out of the house, or after she has sold the house and is living in a far less costly home or apartment; is the amount of alimony and support to be based at all upon the husband's changing income and/or assets, and if so to what extent?

(f) Children: Does the support for the children cease upon their becoming twenty-one; upon their finishing college or postgraduate work; upon their entry into the Armed forces; upon their becoming employed part time or full time. What happens when a child, who marries before the age of twenty-one, later divorces or separates, or if an employed child quits or loses his or her employment? What happens if the wife's remarriage is declared void or is annulled; does the wife's alimony or the children's support cease upon the death of the wife or the death of the husband; is the children's support to be paid solely to the wife or are some of the children's expenses (such as those for college or for a son's clothes) to be paid directly by the father; are expenses of college and camp to be borne by the father, the mother, or partially by both or should the parties' obligations to pay for such expenses be dependent upon the father's or the mother's, or their joint, incomes and assets in the future; who pays for the wife's and children's medical, dental, psychiatric expenses; who has the right to designate physicians and specialists; what about extraordinary medical expenses such as surgery, orthodontia, or encounter therapy at Big Sur?

(g) Discharge of debts: Who pays for what debts of the parties which have accumulated until the signing of the agreement?

° Sometimes alimony is used to include support of both wife and children, and sometimes it is considered solely as support for the wife.

HUSBAND: I don't mind going to the cleaners, but I'll be damned if I'll pay one cent of the $3000 in bills she ran up because Lawyer Toughguy told her to put the screws to me.

LAWYER TOUGHGUY: Don't take everything so personally.

HUSBAND: I ought to punch you . . .

HUSBAND'S LAWYER: I told you, Lawyer Toughguy, that was a dirty trick. She didn't need the chinchilla nightgown and my client won't pay for it.

WIFE (*to* HUSBAND'S LAWYER): You mean I'm going to have to pay for that?

HUSBAND'S LAWYER: How many women own chincilla nightgowns? You will be the rage of the Beautiful People.

WIFE: On $125 a week?

LAWYER TOUGHGUY: Everybody's got to compromise.

(h) Income tax provisions: It is a frequent inducement to the husband, if the wife agrees, to sign joint tax returns for past years. Where she does agree, she should be indemnified against any past or future tax liability, including all assessments and penalties. The agreement should further provide which of the parties is to receive the exemption provided by the tax laws for each of the children.

(i) Life insurance: The amount of life insurance, and whether the wife and/or the children are beneficiaries, who owns the policies and who pays the premiums, must be provided for; what happens to such insurance where the wife remarries or dies before her husband should also be considered, and the parties should determine and state what they intend the tax consequences shall be when and if such proceeds are received.

(j) Counsel fees: Who pays the wife's lawyer, husband or wife? Does the wife indemnify the husband against charges for other lawyers employed by her? The tax consequences of provisions relating to counsel fees are also complicated and should be considered carefully by the clients.

There is a good deal of other "boiler-plate" (roughly standard, but necessary) language which goes into many separation agreements and which has special and important meanings.

Many agreements contain provisions for arbitration. Some contain terms providing for the payment of the wife's counsel fees, should she have to sue to collect alimony or support. Many agreements specify minimum provisions to be inserted in each other's wills, and others provide for the creation of different sorts of trust agreements for the benefit of the wife and/or children. Some agreements expressly set forth as exhibits such information as the husband's income tax return and other financial statements to prevent future quarreling over representations that were made at the time the agreement was executed.

Each agreement carries a provision as to whether it will be incorporated into a subsequent decree of separation or divorce, if such a decree is granted, and whether the agreement is merged into such a decree and whether it shall survive it. The consequences of these provisions vary from state to state, and are of considerable importance. Separation agreements, like ordinary commercial agreements, are often no better than the people who are parties to them. The embittered wife, who "takes" her husband, often finds that the result of her matrimonial Munich is nothing but a piece of paper that cannot be enforced because the husband simply cannot afford it. Husbands who cow their wives and force them one way or another to accept too little for themselves or the children, find that they have bought decades of litigation and counsel fees. Lawyers have an obligation to try to prevent these contractual catastrophes, and they are better handled before the "Thirty Years' War," not afterward.

CHAPTER 9

Matrimonial Trials:
Facts and Fiction

We consider here what happens during contested matrimonial trials. Uncontested trials are simply *pro forma* scraps run through by attorneys and their clients, who have already agreed upon the grounds that will be used and upon the terms of settlement that the court will be urged to rubber-stamp.

As we have already pointed out, to have reached the courthouse steps is to proclaim that somebody has already goofed. Why lawyers and clients in the weeks and months before trial cannot come to a more realistic judgment than a judge, who will spend much less time on the case, is hard to explain. Either the clients or the lawyers, or both, were unreasonable, niggardly, spiteful, and/or stupid.

Judges, knowing all this, are often impatient, curt, irascible, or just plain bored. They are truly, and perhaps properly, resentful that our prisons are overcrowded with men and women who cannot have their day in court because there are too few judges. They are annoyed that they have to sit and listen to the same old malarkey while far more interesting and novel cases are being assigned to other judges. And they know darned well that their job is primarily to sift through vengeful, accusatory bickering, to do the bookkeeping which two lawyers and two clients, and perhaps some accountants, could not do for themselves.

Obviously this is not always true. Fascinating new questions of law frequently come up, and sometimes the spouses and their counsel have earnestly tried to reach an accord, but require an objective determination by the judge. And the fact is that regardless of the law on the books, we are in an age where we do, and should, recognize that dead marriages should be dissolved without the necessity of the hocus-pocus of matrimonial accusations and counteraccusations.

Usually, the judge recognizes that his function is really to arbitrate between conflicting contentions as to what is a fair and equitable division of property and income.*

And so, just as in the movies and on TV, the parties, their attorneys, their witnesses (and sometimes the children) arrive in court. The glaring, the sobs, the grimaces and the hatred are all there, but from this point on the resemblance to what happens in the media is very slight indeed.

Usually both counsel (without clients and witnesses) are invited into the judges chambers.

WIFE'S LAWYER (*after the amenities*): Your Honor, in twenty years of matrimonial practice I have never encountered such a penurious husband, and one who, I might add, is not only loaded but has treated my client like a dog.

HUSBAND'S LAWYER: Sir, when you hear the facts in this case, not only will you throw this witch out of court but you may want to take custody of the children from her.

JUDGE (*stifling a yawn, pencil at the ready*): Gentlemen, how much?

WIFE'S LAWYER: Judge, this guy has got money hidden in so many places that it would take a team of accountants . . .

HUSBAND'S LAWYER: My client is on the skids, Judge. The wife doesn't want to understand that the party is over, not only for her, but for both of them.

* Some thirty states permit the court, in its discretion, to award property and alimony. In community property states, most property acquired during marriage is owned jointly, but, depending upon the state, may under certain circumstances be unequally divided upon divorce. See the excellent discussion of varying property rights of spouses by Julia Perles: "Allocation of Property Rights upon Divorce," N.Y.L.J., December 28, 1971.

JUDGE (*full yawn*): I haven't got all day. How much?

WIFE'S LAWYER: You see, sir, this case is different . . .

JUDGE: Damn it, I'm not on the bench and you aren't performing for your clients. How much?

WIFE'S LAWYER: She is only asking for $250 a week for her and the children, two lovely little kids . . .

JUDGE (*after asking a batch of sensible questions, such as the ages of the parties, their occupations, the ages of the children, and what the husband's tax returns show*): Come on, Counselor, they have only been married five years, your client works part time, the husband is employed by a well-known public company, and he only earns $18,000 a year.

WIFE'S LAWYER (*perspiration on brow*): Judge, during that five years this guy has had three different girl friends.

JUDGE: Maybe when I see the wife I will know why. Come up with a reasonable request.

HUSBAND'S LAWYER: Judge, my client is deeply in debt and he is probably going to be fired.

JUDGE: When he gets fired, come back and we will give you some relief. In the meanwhile, he's got to take care of his kids, and the kids need a mother. What are you offering?

HUSBAND'S LAWYER: Seventy-five a week, and I think . . .

And so it goes. Very often the judge tries to strike a balance and suggests a figure. Sometimes he talks to the lawyers separately. Sometimes he talks to the lawyers and the clients. Very often, he throws up his hands in disgust and decides that it will be less trouble to try the case. Sometimes lawyers get the feeling that their case is lost before it begins. Sometimes the judge gets to the nub of the matter very quickly.

Take another case:

JUDGE: Now listen, Counselor, you can try this case if you want to, but I'm telling you right now I don't like twenty-two-year-old girls who marry sixty-five-year-old men. I especially don't like them when they sue for divorce after six months. I don't think I am going to be impressed by the "she-tried-to-make-a-go-of-it" routine, and if I were you, I would take the settlement and run like, if you will pardon the expression, a thief.

WIFE'S LAWYER (*running like, if you will pardon the expression, a thief*): Perhaps Your Honor is right in view of the fact that she could go back to modeling. Perhaps I should try again to see if I can convince her.

JUDGE: What kind of modeling did she do?

HUSBAND'S LAWYER: I have some very interesting pictures, right here—

JUDGE: Never mind. Why don't we get rid of this case?

By the time of trial, almost all husbands and wives have accommodated themselves to the fact that the marriage is over. It is the "how much" which remains in dispute.

Even among the rare cases which go all the way to the courthouse, up its stairs, and through several unproductive settlement attempts by the judge, few go through a trial of all the issues pleaded by the lawyers. What usually happens is that the husband's lawyer withdraws his client's defense to the wife's complaint and states that his client wishes only to defend the case on the issues of finances.

HUSBAND: Bullshit, I want to fight her all the way. She can never prove I mistreated her or the kids.

HUSBAND'S LAWYER: If she loses, she's still married to you. I thought you had a new girl you were interested in?

HUSBAND: But, if I give in on her cruelty charges won't the judge hold it against me in considering how much to award?

The answer to the husband's question is tricky. The judge knows and expects that the defense to the wife's charges of adultery or cruelty will be withdrawn. He knows that they were either true, half true, or completely fabricated by the wife to gain her freedom (or to get rid of a guy who wanted his), and usually he pays no attention to the proof in undefended cases. And usually where the husband's lawyer withdraws his defense, it is by prearrangement with the wife's lawyer and on the "gentlemen's understanding" that the least innocuous charges in the

complaint will be proven: Just enough to satisfy the state statute
and the court that "grounds" exist. But lawyers are, and should
be, careful that what is proven in these partially defended cases
doesn't contain matter which will poison the court's mind in deciding the financial issues.

WIFE: (*testifying to prove her case*): For example, he won't let
the children play with blacks, Italians, Jews or kids whose
parents are poor.
JUDGE: He actually said that to you?
WIFE: Oh, many times.
HUSBAND'S LAWYER: Your Honor, if this is the sort of nonsense
that Mrs. X is going to testify to, I will ask the court to permit
my client to defend this case in its entirety . . .

Yet there are states where the losing wife gets no support and
conversely the winning husband pays none to the wife. There
are states such as New York where the wife may lose and still
receive support, provided she has not committed adultery or has
not been guilty of abandonment or such "cruel and inhuman
treatment" of the husband as would entitle him to a decree of
divorce. There are even states where permanent support for a
wife after a divorce is not allowed or is severely restricted. And
there are people who simply want to go all the way "to the mat"
regardless of the consequences. This may even happen in such
"no-fault" states as California, Michigan, Florida, Texas, New
Jersey, and Iowa; and sometimes in states where, after pro-
scribed waiting periods, it is sufficient to show that the marriage is "irretrievably broken," or that there are "irreconcilable
differences" between the parties, or that they have been living
apart (sometimes, as in New York, pursuant to an agreement or
decree of separation) for a specified period of time.

In Florida, for example, where a party may be awarded a divorce at any time by proving that the marriage is "irretrievably
broken," the other party may still seek an order directing either
or both parties "to consult with a marriage counselor, a psychologist or psychiatrist, a minister, a priest, or rabbi, or any other

person deemed qualified by the court and acceptable to the party or parties ordered to seek consultation." So even in that and other no-fault states, a husband or wife trying to get across to the court what a burden the other is, may, by "defense," convey to the court those "relevant" facts that he or she wishes to. It is difficult to prevent by legislation attempts by the so-called "innocent spouse" to propagandize his (or her) grievances and to influence the court in his favor.

In matrimonial litigation, as in other forms of trial work, it is the "white hats" versus "black hats"—the good guys against the bad guys. Where such issues as adultery, abandonment, cruel and inhuman treatment, or alcoholism are involved, opportunities abound for convincing the court of who is the victim and who is the transgressor. The extent to which the court will be influenced by these factors depends on the jurisdiction, the law on its books, and, of course, largely on the personal background of the judge and how he privately views marriage and divorce.

Where only the finances of the parties are in issue the court will still be swayed by its own evaluation of the parties, and the skill with which the respective lawyers glorify their clients and denigrate their "opponents."

WIFE's LAWYER: The year before you left your wife, your tax return showed $10,000 in income, the same as this year, right?
HUSBAND: Yes.
LAWYER: And last year you spent on yourself, your wife, and the children over $19,000 according to these canceled checks and bank statements.
HUSBAND: Yes.
LAWYER: And even managed, last year, to have a cleaning woman three times a week and two cars?
HUSBAND: Yes, I told you, I work for my father and when he found out about this divorce and the style my wife and I were living on, he stopped giving me the right to charge for extras, took away the company car, and stopped my expense account.
WIFE's LAWYER: And during the last year your father's business has not gotten any worse; indeed, it has improved?

HUSBAND'S LAWYER: Objection, Your Honor, the father's business ability is not relevant nor does a father have to support his daughter-in-law.

JUDGE A: Yes, yes, come along Counselor, this lady has to learn that the party is over. I'm not going to direct that her father-in-law support her. Maybe the father-in-law doesn't like her. I'm not going to spend all day looking into that sort of question."

But

JUDGE B: Your objection is overruled. I want to know whether the father is cooperating with his son for the purpose of this squabble. If the husband here is financially less able because he and his father want him to appear to be doing financially worse, then I will take that into consideration.

Or

WIFE'S LAWYER: You took the children with Miss X to the "21" Club for dinner?

HUSBAND: Yes.

WIFE'S LAWYER: You spent over $75 on that occasion?

HUSBAND'S LAWYER: Objection, Your Honor . . .

JUDGE A: I think this is disgraceful. Before you even find out whether you're free, you are already introducing these young children to another woman and all this while you want the court to go tell your wife of twenty years to go out and get a job!

And yet another reaction

JUDGE B: Sustained. This couple has been living apart for several months. The husband doesn't have to live like a monk. As I understand it, this was some sort of a party for the young son . . .

WIFE'S LAWYER: My client can't afford to throw parties for her children at luxurious restaurants . . .

JUDGE B: "Come, come, Counselor, your client isn't going to be rewarded because her husband felt a little expansive about his son one night.

WIFE'S LAWYER: Expansive about the son or Miss X, Judge?

JUDGE B: I said the objection is sustained.

The examples are endless, the object is the same: place the client in the best light possible. Make the court want to award the most support for the wife and children or the least, depending on whom the lawyer represents. It is at the trial where the wife, who has used all the credit cards, refused to make the husband's bed, called his employer, poisoned the children's minds, refused the husband's visitation, etc., suffers. Now she must find reasons for her conduct, and, instead of prosecuting her husband, she must defend her own and her lawyer's tactics from the time of separation.

And it is at the trial when the husband, who has hidden income and assets, starved out his wife, had her followed by detectives (unproductively, but expensively), hired Lawyer Toughguy, abused visitation privileges, sent money late too often, called the wife's friends or employers, etc., similarly suffers.

LAWYER TOUGHGUY: Madam, you have been seeing Mr. X, regularly?

WIFE: Yes.

LAWYER TOUGHGUY: Had dinner with him alone several times?

JUDGE: Why shouldn't she have? Your client wasn't supporting her. Maybe she needed a meal?

LAWYER TOUGHGUY: You'll see this woman had a lot more going than free meals, Judge.

JUDGE: You better have plenty of proof, Counselor. From where I sit this woman needed all the friends she could get with the sort of treatment she was getting from your client.

LAWYER TOUGHGUY We have detectives who will show you that she was still "having dinner" with Mr. X at five a.m.

JUDGE: Your client has money for detectives but not for his kids? Maybe I won't believe them. Maybe this woman spent the evening begging for money for herself and her children. Maybe she was sick. We'll see. Of course, I'll listen to all the evidence . . .

LAWYER TOUGHGUY: *Gulp.*

On and on it goes. The witnesses testify to corroborate and deny "guilt." The accountants and parties testify about their standard of living; their current needs. The husband (even one who is sincere) forecasts bad business, tenuous relationships with his employers, the need for a decent standard of living for himself in order to insure a future which will permit him to support the wife and children. The wife (even one who is sincere) forecasts that as she and the children get older their needs will increase. The children's clothes will cost more, the rent will continue to go up, the children must be educated, the necessary medical and dental work so long postponed must be taken care of as must the back bills. As the contestants put their future on the block, the human devastation of the family unit is aired before a court which, with usually too little time and too few facts, must make an extraordinarily difficult decision: how to divide too little among ex-lovers and their children. Even if the court were not compelled to make its Hobson's choice after only knowing the parties briefly in a surrounding unsettling, unfamiliar, and sometimes terrifying to them, its task is not simple. But to expect justice where the situation is exacerbated by months of anxiety, tension, and acrimony is to expect far too much.

The division of the income that one family is barely able to live on between what is about to become two families is too delicate to be left to the trial process as it presently exists. Many courts now require the parties to submit, in advance of trial, budgets of projected needs and statements of finances by the parties. But these documents, when filled out by the clients and their advocates, reflect the exaggerations and distortions of the parties' accusations more than the truth. Many, if not most, wives lack the information the court needs. Many husbands are reluctant to make the information available until it is too late to be thoroughly digested by the court. And bookkeeping and fiscal sleuthing is not a favorite judicial pastime.

Specialized family courts are emerging in many states, with staffs theoretically able to meet the complexities of modern matrimonial strife. Courts and legislators are responding to demands for change and reform. But the very nature of matrimonial bickering and the steadily increasing case loads in jurisdictions where divorce rates are high, thwart genuine attempts to provide the atmosphere, trained judges, psychologists, accountants, and others necessary to make the courtroom a sensible place to settle marital convulsions.

Because of the peculiarities of different laws among the states it is sometimes (at least theoretically), to the advantage of some husbands to proceed to trial rather than settle. In New York for example (as in some other states) the court lacks the power to award a husband's capital assets to the wife, even where a husband got his start in business from funds borrowed from his wife or her parents; and even where the husband has dissuaded the wife, over a period of decades, from pursuing her own career. Under those circumstances it is a wonder that the great majority of cases where the husband's capital assets largely exceed the wife's are settled in New York, with the wife receiving a portion of the husband's assets. Part of the reason is that many husbands realize the inequity and make more favorable settlements than they have to. Another reason is that they are fearful that the judge will take into account the disproportionate distribution of assets and will "clobber" the husband with a disproportionately high allowance for support of the wife and children.

In order to avoid the rigors of trial and to achieve a speedy determination, and in order to overcome their own or their lawyers' inability to agree to the terms of a settlement, parties sometimes submit their controversy to arbitration. Arbitration is a rather informal proceeding by which the parties either select or have selected for them nonjudicial arbitrators (usually between one and three) who determine the controversy and make "an award" upon which a subsequent judgment may then be entered. Arbitrators, who are sometimes lawyers but who need not be, frequently ignore and do not feel bound by strict rules of evidence, and they tend to make their determinations in accordance with what they feel is just and fair and without regard to judicial precedent (i.e., what other courts have decided in similar circumstances).

The flexibility of arbitration is considered by many lawyers to be its greatest weakness since it is extremely difficult to appeal from an adverse determination even where arbitrators blatantly fail to apply customary principles of law or where they ignore facts which would be persuasive in a court of law. Generally, arbitration awards will be set aside by courts only where the arbitrators have shown bias or have been guilty of gross misconduct. Because of the finality and nonappealability of most arbitration awards, and the reluctance of most lawyers to try their cases before strangers, few matrimonial disputes are disposed of in arbitration. Further, not all issues (for example, those relating to the custody of children) are arbitrable in the view of some courts. Consequently, in these jurisdictions this informal method of trial is unavailable. Of course, arbitrators cannot award a divorce, separation, or annulment to any party.

Effective matrimonial trial lawyers are not screamers nor do they get very far venting bile toward their opponent or his client. There is a significant difference between what a client at trial wants his lawyer to say and what a judge wants to hear. Lawyers too often try their cases to please their clients, because they know how desperately these husbands and wives have waited for the day of reckoning.

But there is no such day for the court, which wants to hear reason and logic. Each lawyer has a reservoir of credibility with the court; and exaggerated diatribe and unhelpful invective serves only to diminish it. The most effective trial lawyers are well prepared, low keyed, and sincere advocates of their clients' position. While they may express shock and disbelief at the testimony of their opponent's witnesses, and while they should be relentless in cross-examining witnesses, they should nevertheless, not give the impression that they are gleeful about their opponents discomfiture. Courts and juries do not wish to enter into family squabbles but rather to arbitrate them dispassionately. The impression that the trial lawyer must convey to the court should be of a sense of sorrow rather than ferocity.

An attorney representing the wife might begin his opening address to the jury as follows: "Ladies and gentlemen, we are embarked today and together on an unhappy project. It is, unfortunately, our task to determine whether a marriage of twenty years should be terminated. As you will see, my client has done everything in her power and would continue to do everything in her power to make your job unnecessary, but my client cannot hold her marriage together by herself or even with the aid of three lovely children. She requires, if not the love of her husband, at least his understanding. As you will see, my client expects and wants only justice at your hands; she does not ask and does not expect revenge. The evidence will show that my client, for her sake, for the sake of these children, and, no doubt, even for the sake of this husband, requires that an end be put to this desperately unhappy relationship. It will show . . ."

The tone of that address is probably a good deal more effective than that adopted by a more militant lawyer: "Good morning, ladies and gentlemen. Simply put, this case involves an attempt by my client to free herself after twenty years from a bum who throughout the marriage has been browbeating her until she hardly knows her name. Adultery? Cruelty? Viciousness? You will hear it all in sickening detail. You are called upon to sit in judgment upon a man who has mistreated his wife and children in a manner which we simply will not tolerate. We will show you . . ."

While much criticism has been made of the conduct of lawyers in today's judicial process, too little has been said of the risks that litigants run when they face the intractable, opinionated, and/or authoritarian judge before whom an impartial trial is impossible.

The irascible judge is not such a rarity that the possibility of having one's fate consigned to his judgment should be ignored. Judges are more often than not political animals, and although that fact alone does not disqualify them, too many are the victims of their own cynicism about the very process which created their jobs, and lack the qualities necessary to make impartial decisions. And since judges are appointed or elected in their middle and later years, they often hold views at odds with those whom they judge. This explains why lawyers urge, when they should not have to, that husbands cut their hair, that wives wear plain black dresses, and that all clients conduct themselves in a manner which will appeal to the judge rather than in a way in which they will feel most at ease.

Few trial lawyers would argue that many well-prepared and highly deserving claims or defenses have been decimated by trial judges whose disruptive and pre-emptory rulings have made a fair trial impossible. The same lawyers, fearful of judicial retribution by the same judges before whom they appear day after day, will not, for obvious reasons, publicize their feelings.

In matters matrimonial some judges are notoriously pro-husband; others pro-wife. Some are pro some lawyers and against others. Some jurists hate presiding over matrimonial cases altogether. Others treat these cases as "stepchildren" and postpone them or try them piecemeal so that the results cannot help but be adversely affected.

We have referred before to the fact that many judges permit their personal experiences, predilections, or prejudices to become involved in cases where the facts and circumstances are alien to their own experience. Consider, for instance, the recent predicament of Burton I. Monasch, an able New York matrimonial lawyer who represented a wife seeking alimony from a husband who earned $250,000 per year. The lady testified that her needs included $3500 per year for clothing, an amount consistent with what she had spent while living with her husband. The judge then interjected his own experience and attitude in the following colloquy:

THE COURT: Sir . . . I don't think that my wife and I together, in all our years of marriage, spent so much as that all together. I hate to say it, but it's true.

MR. MONASCH: But Your Honor, I don't think that's relevant . . .

THE COURT: I know. But I earn more than she does and always have [referring to the interim alimony award].

MR. MONASCH: But you don't earn more than the husband does.

THE COURT: No.

MR. MONASCH: And isn't he the one that's responsible?

The relevance of judges' experiences with their own wives is very difficult to keep out of a trial. One can only speculate on how many wives, whose husbands can well afford it, have been denied money for gardening by judges who live in city apartments; for dog-bathing by judges who hate pets; for mah-jongg lessons by judges whose wives work, and for far less frivolous "necessities" by judges who fought with their wives the night before the trial.

Most judges, of course, do not have the hang-ups considered here, and many are well known for their patience and understanding in matrimonial cases. But there is a terrible risk that *your* judge, for one reason or another, will bring disabling and unfair prejudices and attitudes to bear. And this caveat should give further pause to those who play matrimonial "chicken" to the wire.

It should finally be noted that with very rare exceptions, as for example, where unique questions of law are involved, the lawyer who claims to have "won" a matrimonial case or claims to have beaten his opponent, is more often than not "painting the lily"; or, more accurately, just plain lying. It is usually the intention of one lawyer or the other "to lose the case" in the sense that it is anticipated and expected that one party or another (in some jurisdictions, both parties) will be granted a divorce or separation. The trial is almost always geared to settling the issue of "how much" and rarely does either side get or give what they intended to.

CHAPTER 10

Modification of Agreements and Decrees

The rules, statutes, and decisions concerning when and under what circumstances decrees of separation or divorce and agreements of separation may be modified are extremely technical, widely divergent among the states, constantly changing, and difficult to comprehend—even for lawyers. It is a matter of no small concern to husbands and wives to know what their rights are when circumstances change. What happens when the wife and children need more than could be foreseen at the time of agreement or at the time of trial? What happens when the husband can afford to pay less than he had contemplated?

Although it is difficult to generalize about these important questions, it is safe to say that under some circumstances and in some states, courts can and will provide relief. The rule to be applied not only depends upon the law of a particular state but also on whether we are dealing solely with a separation agreement (in which case relief is extremely limited in most states); with an agreement which has been "merged" (roughly, incorporated) into a decree of separation or divorce; or with an agreement which "survives" (roughly, exists apart from or in addition to) the decree of separation or divorce.

Florida,* for example, provides that separation agreements **

* Section 61.14, Florida Statutes.
** It is arguable that this provision violates Constitutional limitations against laws "impairing the Obligation of Contracts." United States Constitution, Article 1, Section 10.

as well as decrees of divorce or separate maintenance may be modified upward or downward "as equity requires with due regard to the changed circumstances and the financial ability of the parties"; and even further provides—unlike many state statutes—that the court may reduce alimony or child support regardless of whether or not arrears which have accrued have been paid.

In New York, on the other hand, where a separation agreement is in effect and is legally valid, no court may change its terms, although relief may be given in a separate proceeding to a wife "in dire need" or likely to become a public charge. A similar rule exists in New York where there exists a separation agreement which has not been merged into a decree of separation or divorce.

And, in New York, as in other states, when no separation agreement exists, the court does have the authority to modify upward or downward its own decrees. Different rules, however, obtain in seeking increased or decreased support obligations for children who are not parties to the agreement.

We assure you that what we have just outlined is a necessary simplification of a labyrinthine network of complicated rules. But the nature of the rules in a particular jurisdiction concerning the subject of modification may be of critical importance to both husbands and wives, and should be explored fully before parties make their agreements or before they risk trial in states which do not permit such modification.

Regardless of the law on the books of any jurisdiction, even where relief can be obtained because of changed circumstances, it must be emphasized that it is not every change in the fortunes of either husband or wife which permits them relief.

Many husbands and wives make a career of applying needlessly and fatuously for relief. After a divorce or separation, the provisions made by the parties are generally intended to bind them, barring unforeseen circumstances. The wife does not continue to be the husband's charge, and the fact that his career advances and he makes more money, or that the cost of living goes

up are not sufficient reasons to award a wife more money—
unless, of course, the husband was so poorly off at the time of
the agreement or decree that his contribution could only be
grossly inadequate. And simply because a husband's business
gets slightly worse, or because he remarries, or because he
wishes deliberately to accept employment at a much lower
rate of pay does not warrant a reduction in his obligations.

It is generally assumed that when the parties entered into
their agreement or when the court awarded its decree these
foreseeable factors were taken into consideration.

But the change of circumstances contemplated by those
courts, which grant relief to the wife or the wife and children,
are drastic changes which were unforeseen and reasonably una-
voidable. For example, it has been held that a lawyer's disbar-
ment is an unforeseen circumstance that would entitle him to a
reduction because of his reduced income. Long illness and incapacity to work might justify an increase in support for a wife or
a reduction for the husband. This rule, of course, is less strictly
applied in the case of children—particularly where the husband's ability to provide for them is initially minimal but later
substantially increases.

While rules permitting modification are obviously necessary,
their existence poses a constant threat, particularly to husbands
who want the security of knowing what their obligations will be
in the future so that they can plan for their own separate lives.
These same rules, unfortunately, are often used by vindictive
wives who make applications simply to annoy and harass the
husband and to cause him unnecessary legal expenses.

It seems to us that where the husband is able to provide suitably for his wife and children at the time of the agreement or
decree, it should require an extremely strong showing before the
wife should be entitled to "go back to the well." Where she
abuses the privilege she should have to pay her own counsel
fees and, perhaps, also be required to pay her husband's.

On the other hand, where the agreement or decree, because of
the financial difficulties of the husband at that time was wholly

inadequate to provide for the wife (considering, of course, the usual factors such as duration of the marriage, number and age of children, the preseparation standard of living, etc.), such relief "as justice requires" should be granted. Where a wife has struggled for twenty years with her husband and is left with little money for herself and her children, she should not be penalized by having made an agreement, fair when it was made, but disproportionate to any future prosperity of her husband; even if she is not married to him when he achieves such prosperity. The point, of course, is surely arguable.

CHAPTER 11

Custody of Children

In at least 90 per cent of all matrimonial cases involving children, custody is awarded to the mother, and usually by mutual consent of the parties. In contested cases, we are again met by a variety of different rules, statutes, and decisions among the different states concerning who is the proper custodian for children.

Every decision of every court relating to child custody contains the usual and obvious statement that what the court wishes to do is what is best for the child or children involved. And, as far as sincerity goes, most lawyers would agree that in determining questions of custody, courts are usually at their very best.

At a custody hearing, neither the lawyers nor the clients are rushed, whatever evidence is available from almost any source is eagerly accepted, and no judge is oblivious to the importance of the decision which he is called upon to make.

But judges are human; they are the product of their own upbringing, environment, and background, and they cannot shed their own personal views concerning which of the dozens of factors presented are relevant in determining who shall be given custody.

In the early development of the law, the father was considered the natural guardian of his child, and he was almost always entitled to custody of the children when the parties separated or divorced. Today many states, by statute or decision, give husband and wife equal rights to the custody of children; some states, by statute or decision, favor custody in the mother if the children are young or if they are girls; and others favor custody in the father for older boys. But regardless of the state, courts will, uniformly, listen thoughtfully to any evidence which can be produced and will shed light on which parent (or, as we shall see, which third party) would make the more suitable guardian.

A variety of factors is considered by the courts, including the moral conduct of the parties, their emotional and physical status, the comparative environments in which the child or children may be placed, the child's age, health, and sex, the fact that the child or children have become used to and are comfortable in their present surroundings, the possibility that a child's emotional or physical health may be affected by a parent's religious views, the preference expressed by the child, who the "guilty" party is in the separation or divorce proceedings, or who brought about the split-up of the family. Perhaps even more important—although seldom stated as a factor in determining custodial arrangements for children—is the moral code of the particular state or the particular community in which the case is heard. While a parent's political or moral philosophy may be irrelevant to one judge, it may be—and has been— crucial to others. As we shall see, extramarital affairs conducted under circumstances which have not affected or which will not in the future harm children may be irrelevant to some courts, but may bar custody to some parents in others.

Of course, an appreciable number of custody cases arise when one of the parties to a separation agreement becomes dissatisfied with the custodial arrangements they agreed to. Other cases arise where parties having custody of children make—because of emergencies or because of present exigencies—what are intended to be short-term arrangements with their mates or with third parties to change previous custody arrangements; with the understanding that the children will be returned after a period of time or upon the happening of a contingency. Often, the temporary custodian refuses to keep his part of the bargain.

While the agreements reached by parents between themselves and with third parties are relevant, they are by no means conclusive. Children are not parties to such agreements, and courts, mindful of their obligations to infants, will not hesitate to award custody in a manner not in accord with such agreements. A parent who surrenders a child runs the risk of losing its custody and the longer the period of such surrender, the greater the risk.

Certain (almost universal) rules apply in custody cases, regardless of the state involved. One of those rules is that courts are loath to experiment in custody cases and to shift the custody from one parent to another where the child is flourishing in the atmosphere in which it has been placed. As one New York court said (*Matter of Lang* v. *Lang* 9 App. Div. 2d 401), "the custody of infant children is not to be shifted from parent to parent merely because the non-custodial parent has experienced an improvement in condition, status, or character. At least this is true so long as the custodial parent has not been shown to be unfit, or perhaps less fit, to continue to serve as the proper custodian."

In another case (*People ex rel. Fields* v. *Kaufmann*, 9 App. Div. 2d 375), a New York Appellate Court reversed an order granting custody to a mother who had become ill with polio, notwithstanding the rehabilitation shown by the mother over a period of a year, and notwithstanding the fact that she was shortly to assume the directorship of a hospital in Philadelphia under a five-year contract. Having demonstrated to the court that the mother "performed a miracle of self-rehabilitation" and that she deserved great credit "for her achievement," the court concluded that the mother had not produced enough evidence to warrant the shifting of custody to her, and directed a further hearing.

Upon the rehearing, the trial court (27 Misc. 2d 625), again noting the mother's "terrible ordeal . . . in a remarkable struggle for rehabilitation," still found that permanent custody should be awarded to the father "who has not shirked or impaired the responsibility for the care and custody of the children, which has been cast wholly upon him during the past six years, virtually since they were born."

Courts throughout the United States pay particular attention to the moral climate in which children live. How "moral climate" is defined, however, varies from fairly flexible to incredibly rigid, backward, self-righteous, and asinine in the light of any fair application of modern psychiatric and sociological standards. As in perhaps most states, New York recognizes a flexible standard by which moral transgressions are weighed in the light of their effect upon children and not upon how right or wrong the court regards them in a vacuum. In one case, for example (*Bunim* v. *Bunim,* 298 N.Y. 391), the trial court had awarded custody to a mother who not only committeed adultery on several occasions but who espoused a doctrine of marital infidelity which could not help but affect young children living with her. New York's highest court reversed that determination, saying:

On the trial of this divorce suit the wife admitted numerous deliberate adulteries (with a man who was married and had children), attempted to rationalize and justify those adulteries, denied any repentence therefor, commited perjury in swearing to denials in her answer (see Civ. Prac. Act, § 1148), and, as found by both courts below, testified to a deliberately false story as to consent by plaintiff (a reputable and successful physician) to the adulteries. With all that in the record, custody of the two children of the marriage (eleven and thirteen years old at the time of the trial) has been, nonetheless, awarded to defendant.

There is an affirmed finding below that the husband is a fit and proper person to have such custody, and no such finding as to the wife, but a finding that "the interests and welfare of the children, the issue of said marriage, will be best served by awarding the custody to the defendant." We see in this record no conceivable basis for that latter finding, unless it be the testimony of the two daughters that, though they love their father, they prefer to live with their mother. Unless that attitude of these adolescent girls be controlling as against every other fact and consideration (see, contra, *People ex rel. Glendening v. Glendening,* 259 App. Div. 384, affd. 284 N.Y. 598), this judgment, insofar as it deals with custody, is unsupported and unsupportable.

No decision by any court can restore this broken home or give these children what they need and have a right to—the care and protection of two dutiful parents. No court welcomes such problems, or feels at ease in deciding them. But a decision there must be, and it cannot be one repugnant to all normal concepts of sex, family and marriage. The State of New York has old, strong policies on those subjects, strongly stated by the Legislature (see, for instance, Penal Law, § 100; Civ. Prac. Act, § 1147, 1161, 1170; Domestic Relations Law, § 8). Our whole society is based on the absolutely fundamental proposition that: "Marriage, as creating the most important relation in life," has "more to do with the morals and civilization of a people than any other institution" (*Maynard v. Hill,* 125 U.S. 190, 205). Defendant here, in open court, has stated her considered belief in the propriety of indulgence, by a dissatisfied wife such as herself, in extramarital sex experimentation. It cannot be that "the best interests and welfare" of those impressionable teen-age girls will be "best served" by awarding their custody to one who proclaims, and lives by, such extraordinary ideas of right conduct.

Other courts in New York and elsewhere have treated adultery flexibly and sensibly and, while not recommending it, have still awarded custody to the mother in those instances where the mother's conduct has not influenced and is not likely to affect the children. For example, where the mother's sexual appetites are satisfied outside the home, where the children are not left alone, and where the mother does not spend long periods of time away from them, her conduct need not act as a bar to her custody of infants.

At the other end of the spectrum, we have good old Nebraska.

That state stands alone as being the only one where adultery by the mother in and of itself and regardless of the circumstances constitutes, as a matter of law, a bar to her being awarded custody provided that it is found that the husband is fit to have such custody. As the Nebraska court said (in *Yost* v. *Yost*, 161 Neb. 164, 173–74), "She [the mother] has forfeited any right she may have had to the custody of her children because of her disgraceful conduct. One may not willfully destroy the family relationship as she has done and expect a court to give consideration to her to the detriment of the husband she has so grievously wronged."

Maryland, on the other hand, has created an interesting legal presumption concerning the wife who commits adultery. It merely assumes that the wife is a horrible harridan, unworthy of custody, but permits her to make a "strong showing . . . to overcome the usual rule against awarding custody to an adulterous mother." And so, for example, in *Bray* v. *Bray*, 171 A.2d 500, the court said:

> Although somewhat repetitious, it seems clear from these decisions and the authorities cited therein, as well as any number of previous decisions of this Court, that the primary consideration of the Court in a custody case is the welfare of the child, and each case must be determined by its own particular facts. There are many factors that may properly be considered in determining what are the best interests and welfare of a child, when its custody is involved. Among these is the fact, if shown, that its mother has committed adultery. The fact that she has committed adultery does not constitute an absolute and inflexible bar to her being awarded custody (221 Md. 358, 157 A. 2d 447; 222 Md. 75, 158 A. 2d 610, for when the adulterous relationship has ceased for a reasonable period of time, so as to render it unlikely that it will be revived, and the mother has changed her way of living and demonstrates that she is a fit and proper person to raise her child in a clean and wholesome moral atmosphere, then her past indiscretions may be overlooked in considering the award of custody. But, when it is shown that the mother has committed adultery, the courts

in this state (see the long line of Maryland cases cited in foot-note 4 of the Hild case) and elsewhere usually award the cus-tody of the children to the innocent party (provided he be a fit and proper person), not as a punishment or reward, but upon the assumption, which bears directly on the children's welfare, that they will be reared in cleaner and more whole-some moral surroundings. And the mother, who has been shown to have committed adultery and who claims to have mended her ways and to be a fit and proper person to raise a child, must make "a strong showing" to overcome the usual rule against awarding custody to an adulterous mother; and, although the fact that she has subsequently married her para-mour may be considered in determining her fitness, it, alone, will not be regarded as meeting the requirements of such a showing.

In the case at bar, the appellant makes no attempt at a "strong showing" to overcome the usual rule. As far as the rec-ord discloses, she contents herself with a showing that she has married her paramour, is living in, perhaps, a slightly larger house than the father, and that the child is receiving good care physically. The chancellor found that the child would receive proper care in the custody of her father, to whom he awarded custody, and we are unable to say that his ruling was erroneous.

Order affirmed, with costs. (at pp. 504–505)

The Maryland case is particularly interesting since it treated the wife's "redemption" by the marrying of her paramour as of no avail, while another court in Louisiana regarded the very fact of subsequent marriage to the paramour as being the saving grace in permitting an adulterous mother to retain custody of her infant. So, in *Wade* v. *Wade*, 129 So.2d 571, the court said:

The defendant-father appeals from the award of the care and custody of his three-year-old minor son to the plaintiff-mother, following a judgment of separation from bed and board, on the ground of abandonment, obtained by the mother. The fa-ther charges the mother is morally unfit because she lived openly as the concubine of another man, before obtaining her divorce, and bore him a child. This the mother frankly admitted. However, after obtaining her final divorce, she married her paramour.

At the time of the hearing, the District Judge was first inclined to award the custody to the father, but suggested the mother might redeem herself by contracting marriage with her paramour. All parties in open Court, during oral argument here, stipulated that the mother obtained a final divorce, married her paramour and he is supporting her and the child adequately. The father, following his abandonment of his wife and child, seldom saw the child, and contributed little or nothing to their support.

Our jurisprudence is too well settled, to admit of doubt, that the paramount consideration in determining which parent is entitled to the custody, after divorce, is the welfare and best interest of the child. Under this rule, minor children have been consistently awarded to the mother unless she has been found morally unfit or incapable of caring for them.

Accordingly, the mother, though guilty of immoral conduct, can redeem herself by returning to the path of rectitude. The mother here has done so by contracting marriage with her paramour. Since there is no evidence that her home is now an unfit place for the child, we see no reason to disagree with the Trial Court. Therefore, the award of custody to the mother is affirmed, costs in both Courts to be paid by defendant-appellant.

Affirmed. (at p. 572)

When will some of our courts learn that many of us do not live by the Scriptures? We are a nation not only of many races, colors, and creeds, but of men and women whose philosophies, ideologies, and conduct run the full spectrum of human thought and behavior. But many courts make no allowance for the heathen among us, for the impulsive among us, for the political maverick among us, for the nonconformist among us.

Consider how those in the latter group would flourish in Missouri, where, in words harking back to *The Scarlet Letter*, the

Appellate Court in *L——* v. *N——*, 326 S.W. 2d 751, had the following to say:

> As we enter upon the unwelcome and unpleasant duty of writing the closing chapter in another sordid story of marital discord and dissolution, we draw a charitable cloak of anonymity about the actors that two innocent little girls, whose custody is in issue, may not be scourged in years to come by a recorded recital of the sin and shame of their mother. On this appeal by the wife and mother from a decree dismissing her petition and awarding to the husband and father a divorce . . . and the custody of the two girls, the older born on November 20, 1950, and the younger born on September 23, 1954. . . .
>
> The parties took their marriage vows, "till death do us part," on March 12, 1948. The husband was then twenty-one years of age, the wife younger although her exact age is not disclosed to us. About one year and nine months later, i.e., on December 19, 1949, they separated. The primary, if not sole, cause of that separation (as well as subsequent trouble after the parties resumed habitation under the same roof on June 19, 1950) was an "affair" between the wife and her second cousin. It is apparent from letter exhibits that the wife and her cousin had been "going with each other" before the wife married. At some time not fixed in evidence, the cousin entered military service and, by the Fall of 1949, was airmailing to the wife sultry, romantic letters from his post of duty in Japan. Both of the samples in evidence (admittedly received by the wife) saluted her as "Dearest Darling," both began "Received your letter today," both pledged his intense, inexpressible and inextinguishable love for the wife, and both expressed a burning desire for her and a sustaining hope that they might be married. That his illicit blandishments and licentious endearments did not fall on deaf or unreceptive ears is indicated by his letter of September 17, 1949, in which he promised to "write to you [the wife] every day I can" because "you asked me to write to you every day." And, in the same letter, the cousin adjured her to "just be ready by Xmas," promised that "we will make up for all the time that we

should have been together & wasn't," and told the wife that "when I do get to come home I want you to be free, & if you love me as much as you say you do you will do that for me." . . .

The activities of the cousin during a period of several years after reconciliation of the husband and the wife in June 1950 are concealed by a blind spot in the evidence, but the "affair" between the cousin and the wife again comes into focus some six to eight months before the final separation on February 14, 1958, when the husband "caught them" in an alley. On that occasion, the husband found his automobile parked in the alley, waited until the cousin and the wife (one with an arm around the other and with the younger girl, then less than three years of age, asleep in the seat next to the right door) drove up in another automobile, and then "went over and grabbed him (the cousin) by the shirt collar" and "told him I'd had enough trouble with him and I wanted him to get out and leave me alone." That this had no salutary effect upon the participants in the "affair" is indicated by a letter dated September 9, 1957, from the wife to her sister in St. Louis. In that letter, the wife wrote that "you might see (the cousin) up there—he is going up there to try and get a job—I sure hope he gets one"; and, after informing her sister that the *cousin's* wife (whom he apparently had married after 1950) had obtained a divorce and that the cousin "has to pay her $15 a week," the wife commented that the cousin "needs to get a good job to pay that" and confided that "if (the cousin) gets a good job he wants me to come up there so I will if he does get a good job where I can get by." . . .

Our courts have said frequently that the morals of the respective parents are an appropriate and proper subject of consideration in a custody case. As thus employed, the term "morals" obviously should not be and is not limited to sexual conduct. "Moral law" is "(t)he law of conscience" [Black's *Law Dictionary*, 4th Ed., p. 1160] —"the eternal and indestructable sense of justice and of right written by God on the living tablets of the human heart and revealed in his Holy

Word" [*Moore* v. *Strickling*, 46 W. Va., 515, 33 S.E. 274, 277, 50 L.R.A. 279]; and, "(s)ound morals as taught by the wise men of antiquity, as confirmed by the precepts of the gospel . . . are unchangeable." The same yesterday, today and forever. *Commonwealth of Pennsylvania* v. *Randall*, 183 Pa., Super. 603, 133 A. 2d 276, 279–280. "Morality is a generic term containing the sum total of all . . . moral traits, including honesty, fidelity, peacefulness, etc.," sometimes "referred to as synonymous with character" [*State* v. *Moorman*, 133 Mont. 148, 321 P. 2d 236, 240]; and, we think that the very nature of the overriding principle in cases of this character, i.e., that the welfare of the children is paramount and supreme, dictates and demands that an inquiry into parental "morals" encompass not only sexual conduct but also "common decency, cleanliness of mind and body, honesty, truthfulness, and proper respect for established ideals and institutions, among other things." *State* v. *Clein*, Fla., 93 So. 2d 876, 881.

From time immemorial, truthfulness has been recognized as a cornerstone of morality. One of the Ten Commandments given to Moses on Mount Sinai was the pointed prohibition, "Thou shalt not bear false witness against thy neighbour." Exodus 20:16. In his inspired wisdom, King Solomon declared that "lying lips are abomination to the Lord" [Proverbs 12:22] and twice warned that "a false witness shall not be unpunished, and he that speaketh lies shall not escape." Proverbs 19:5, 9. The word of the Lord through the prophet Zechariah was that "These are the things that ye shall do; Speak ye every man the truth to his neighbour . . ." [Zechariah 8:16]; and, from the apostle Paul came the same ringing command, "Wherefore putting away lying, speak every man truth with his neighbour . . ." Ephesians 4:25. For centuries, perjury has been regarded as an offense involving moral turpitude [*United States* v. *Carrollo*, D.C. Mo., 30 F. Supp. 3, 6]; and, from the founding fathers of our commonwealth whose consciences mayhaps had not become so blunted and inured to half-truths and untruths, there has come down to us tangible statutory evidence of their reverential respect for the divine precepts adjuring truthfulness and condemning falsehood: precepts still accorded diffident lip service but too frequently honored in this day by brazen breach rather than by faithful observance. With truthfulness thus enshrined in the laws of God and of man, how harmonious and how fitting are the declarations of our courts, concerned as they are with the welfare of their wards, that perjury itself demonstrates unfitness to have the care and custody of minor children.

We need not go outside the wife's own testimony in the instant case to ascertain her insolent disdain for the truth. We again note, but pass without further discussion, her testimony concerning the false averments in her verified petition in the second divorce suit brought on her behalf by the *cousin's* mother, as next friend. Then, we observe that, when asked (while on the stand the first time) why she had written the cousin, she promptly answered, "because he was my cousin was the main reason," but that (when recalled) she bluntly denied that she had ever written the cousin while he was in the service, then sandwiched in an equivocal statement that she never wrote "any love letters to him" before returning to a weakened denial that she had written—"not that I remember." As the trial judge took over the questioning, the wife finally said, "I've wrote to him (the cousin), but I didn't think I wrote to him while he was overseas. I guess I did." When interrogated about the letter of September 9, 1957, to her sister in St. Louis, in which the wife had written (while still married to and living with the husband) that "if (the cousin) gets a good job he wants me to come up there so I will if he does get a good job where I can get by," she definitely denied that she and the cousin had been or were in love, blandly "explaining" that the cousin had told her "that he would find a job and help me get by if I couldn't get by up there." However, with the candor we have come to expect of them, the wife's counsel frankly informed us in the course of oral arguments that the wife and the cousin had married while this appeal was pending. See particularly *Watkins* v. *Watkins*, Mo. App., 230 S.W. 2d 778, 783–84.

We recognize that prior misconduct does not *necessarily* require that a mother be denied custody of her children [*Johns* v. *McNabb*, Mo., 247 S.W. 2d 640, 643; *I—— v. B——*,

Mo. App., 305 S.W. 2d 713, 718]; but, the transcript before us not only indicates the mother's gross, habitual and contemptuous disrespect for the moral law but also reflects no evidence of her repentance and rehabilitation. And, without undertaking the needless task of determining whether the wife was guilty of statutory perjury and statutory adultery, the foregoing will suffice to explain what we believe to be the inescapable conclusion that she is a woman of easy virtue and careless truth who has long since forgotten that the price of a virtuous woman "is far above rubies" [Proverbs 31:10] and that, "as a jewel of gold in a swine's snout, so is a fair woman which is without discretion." Proverbs 11:22.

By now, we should have reached an age where our courts should cease arrogating to themselves the function of legislating by judicial fiat what we should read, believe, and think. Yet many custody decisions, when well analyzed, turn not the slightest on how the parents' conduct affects the children, but rather simply focus on the conduct itself and, if found to displease the court, is said to bar one or another parent from custody. A celebrated case of this kind is *Painter* v. *Bannister*, 140 N.W. 2d 152, *cert. denied*, 385 U.S. 949, in which a seventeen-year-old boy's custody, after the death of the mother, was given to maternal grandparents, both sixty years of age, despite, among others, the following considerations:

(a) The explicit finding of the court that the father and mother had a happy marriage.

(b) The court admittedly was not "confronted with a situation where one of the contesting parties is not a fit or proper person."

(c) The questionably sound presumption (questionably asserted in almost every state) of the preference for parents over third parties in matters of custody.

(d) The fact that the mother named her husband as guardian of the child.

(e) The fact that the trial court (which found for the father) had regarded the testimony of the doctor-expert hired by the far wealthier grandparents as "exaggerated."

(f) The fact that the husband had remarried a woman with a master's degree in cinema design, who "apparently likes and has had considerable contact with children." Indeed, the court found that the husband's new wife was anxious to have the child in her house, that she had had considerable contact with children, and that "she would provide a leveling influence" on the husband "and could ably care" for the child.

Nevertheless, Iowa's highest court pointed out a number of factors which led it to conclude that the father should not be awarded custody. Among those factors were:

(a) That the husband "is either an agnostic or atheist and has no concern for formal religious training. He has read a lot of Zen Buddhism. . . ."

(b) The husband was found to be "a political liberal and got into difficulty at a job at the University of Washington for his support of the activities of the American Civil Liberties Union in the university bulletin."

(c) Upon the death of the husband's wife, there were two funerals. One of them was conducted with the husband present alone "in the basement of his home," and the court noted, "He conducted the service and wrote her a long letter." It noted solemnly that the husband attended the church service "in a sport shirt and sweater."

It is interesting to note that subsequently, after the husband lost the case, the grandparents permitted the child to visit him and his new wife in California, and, when he refused to return the child, the grandparents acceded to his wishes and the child remained with the father.

The very strong presumption which exists in favor of parents over third parties has been rightfully criticized although, as proven by the *Painter* case, the rule is not immutable. If the court's quest is for what is best for the child, there are many instances where custody should be granted to relatives or even family agencies as a choice over unfit or unstable parents.°

° See Foster and Freed, "Children and the Law," *Family Law Quarterly*, Volume II, No. 1, March 1968.

Custody, of course, may be taken away from parents so sick, so mentally unstable, so addicted to drugs or alcohol, or so preoccupied with their own lives or problems that the child's welfare could not help but be affected thereby. Again, how much these factors or some combination of them will influence a court depends upon the jurisdiction, but it can be generally said that the better and more frequent test is simply how the children are affected, and, among contestants for the child's custody, who will provide the more stable and the more suitable home.

Children, of course, very often express a preference for one parent or another. The older the child, the more weight his decision will have. Courts are well aware, however, of how often, during custody proceedings, the children are made the pawn and how subject they are to the inducements, threats, or blandishments of the contesting parties. And children have a remarkable facility for recognizing their own power in such proceedings and frequently play their roles to the hilt, pitting one parent against the other and leading the court a merry chase in trying to determine what the children's real desires are.

It is very often true, unfortunately, that custody cases are lost by the parent with the least money. The hiring of investigators, psychiatrists, psychologists, and lawyers familiar with and experienced in custody litigation can be of decisive importance and may lie beyond the means of one of the parties but not the other.

Countless are the cases where the really persuasive and determinative facts are not known or cannot be proven without extensive research and without expert help.

In one case in New York, the attorney-author was consulted by a young husband whose wife was seeking custody of a three-and-one-half-year-old daughter, then residing with the paternal grandparents. The parents had separated approximately one and one-half years previously, and the father had remarried.

The mother, between the time of separation and initiation of the action, had been admitted to two different mental institutions in New York. Each hospitalization was for over a month, and the last discharge had occurred only a few months previous to the wife's attempt to regain custody.

The court, as it frequently does, and with the consent of both attorneys, appointed an independent psychiatrist to examine all of the parties, including the grandparents, the husband, the wife, the child, and the husband's new wife. A short time thereafter, the court psychiatrist rendered a fifteen-page report, and its recommendation was as follows:

> When the mother has properly prepared the home the child can be entrusted in her care. I join those who have advised her to seek long-term psychoanalytically oriented therapy. It is a must that she have appropriate counseling and guidance in regard to rearing and educating the child. This could evolve in the course of her therapy. The child's present preschool experience should not be interrupted if at all possible. I recommend to both concerned families that their primary concern be for the mental health and stability of the child since the bright child is more sensitive and reacts with greater intensity, therefor [sic] is more subject to emotional and mental illness.
>
> The mother's past illness also suggests the need for emotional support, kindness and consideration from those to whom she looks for the same. There is no question but that she had a psychotic-like reaction. There is no indication it is of recurrent nature. Both hospitalizations were related to the one episode of illness.

The report of the court psychiatrist was curious. It indicated (which turned out to be true) that the doctor had not read all of the hospital records in connection with the young mother's hospitalizations, which would have shed light on her conduct following the separation of the parties. The court psychiatrist noted that the mother had moved from hotel to hotel, at times leaving the child alone. It noted that during the wife's pregnancy the wife had gained some forty pounds and that after the parties' separation, the wife took pills and drastically reduced her weight to the point where she weighed ninety pounds prior to her hospitalization. The fact that the wife had taken "excessive amounts of amphetamines prior to her acute episode" was noted. Among the doctor's findings concerning the husband was that "his palms were cold and sweaty" (which leads one to inquire how that particular doctor makes diagnoses in the summer when all of our palms sweat). The psychiatrist's report to the court was taken to an assistant professor of psychiatry at Yale, whose specialty was drugs and drug addiction; and that doctor stated that—based on the report—he was convinced that the young mother was suffering from amphetamine addiction, an extremely serious condition and one which, if borne out by the facts, would clearly contraindicate awarding custody to the mother. The doctor urged that all of the hospital records be made available to him.

When the attorneys appeared before the court, the husband's lawyer asked the court to direct that all hospital records be made available to the husband's expert, and the judge so directed, agreeing that the husband had a right to see those records.

After the records were shown to the husband's expert from Yale, he announced that he was absolutely positive that this young woman, who had had a history of weight reduction and amphetamine consumption dating back long before her pregnancy, had become addicted to that drug. When he interviewed the mother (as the court permitted him to do), she appeared with her lawyer, who treated the husband's doctor as an adversary. The mother refused to produce a urine specimen in order to permit the husband's doctor to determine whether she had recently been taking amphetamines.

The husband's doctor recommended that the mother be followed, since he attributed her present appearance of well-being to the fact that she was being maintained on amphetamines. The mother's hospital history indicated that she had fared poorly in the hospital—with some episodes of violence—and only improved after she had started being released on weekend passes. The doctor reasoned that the mother's improvement was not due to the passage of time or the remission of her illness, but rather to her ability to get pills.

The husband engaged a private investigator who turned up, in no time at all, the doctor who had been dispensing pills to this young lady for many, many years; and further investigation disclosed the names of drugstores where she was filling her prescriptions.

Armed with this data and the lengthy report from the husband's doctor, it became possible to convince the court within two trial days that the wife, indeed, had unwittingly become addicted to amphetamine; that her prognosis was poor without extensive psychiatric treatment; that the child's best interest would be served by leaving her where she was. The court granted liberal visitation privileges to the mother, directed her to lose no more weight, to receive psychiatric treatment, and to have the reports forwarded to the court. It also directed her to submit to examinations at which she was required to submit urine specimens. The court required that those examinations be on such short notice to her that she would be unable to discontinue amphetamine consumption without detection. The court then granted the mother the right, after one year, to seek to regain custody; and made it very clear that, if after that period she did not refrain from her drug habit, the court would award permanent custody to the father.

Subsequently, the mother, by rigid adherence to the court's direction, regained custody of her child. And, perhaps, it may be said that her future happiness, as well as that of her infant's, was due to the fortunate circumstance that her husband and his parents were willing to expend so much money and time in what she and her attorney mistakenly thought was a combat against her, but which turned out to be a struggle against her addiction. And, of course, the real hero of the piece was the husband's psychiatrist.

Often questions of custody depend upon which court or courts have jurisdiction to determine the question. Most states hold that the presence of the child is necessary in order to give the court jurisdiction, and attempts by residents of a state to stash the child in another jurisdiction are usually of no avail. Very often and very tragically, a parent, dissatisfied with the decision concerning custody in one state, takes the child to another jurisdiction. Although this practice is readily recognized by most courts—which are likely to follow the decision of the original court—there have been many cases where "for the best interests of the child," the second state disregards the previous determination of its sister court no matter how recently made. This practice has been widely criticized and leads to endless anguish.

Upon the death of one parent, it is universally held that the surviving parent receives custody unless he or she is proven to be unfit.

Of course, the granting of custody to one parent or another does not give the custodial parent exclusive rights over the welfare of the child. A mother, for example, cannot change the last name of the child to that of a new husband, but she can change the child's religion without the consent of the father. She cannot choose the child's school or make other major decisions without consulting the husband. The court, if it must intervene, will arbitrate the parties' major differences and direct what is best for the child. Ordinarily, however, the court will not interfere in the rational decisions of the parent who has custody.

Courts are reluctant to permit children to be removed from their jurisdiction except for compelling reasons. The remarriage of the wife to a nonresident is sufficiently compelling and will ordinarily be permitted regardless of the terms of a prior separation agreement or decree forbidding the child's removal.

It is extremely difficult to generalize about how flexible or rigid provisions in a separation agreement should be concerning the custody of children. It largely depends upon the parents. Where, for example, the wife has been vindictive and gives every evidence of continuing her past course of vengeance, a too rigid schedule of the husband's visitation privileges may result in his being hauled into court or necessitate his hauling the wife into court over every minor infraction.

WIFE: You were two hours late in picking up Junior last week, so you can't see him this week.
HUSBAND: My car broke down on the highway.
WIFE: The agreement says at ten a.m., and that's what it means. . . .

Or

WIFE: The agreement says weekends and weekends begin on Friday.
HUSBAND: But it's Thanksgiving, and I'd like to take Junior skiing and he has no school on Thursday.
WIFE: The agreement says . . .

It should be apparent that as the children grow older, as they become ill, as the circumstances of the parties change, new and different custodial arrangements should be made, and it is extremely difficult to put in an agreement or a decree all of the rights and privileges associated with visitation that will be applicable for all time. Intelligent spouses recognize this. They specifically provide that from time to time such visitation privileges as are provided may have to be changed.

Where no cooperation is forthcoming from one or both parents, they must return again and again to the court in order to apply for modifications of their arrangements.

The parent who has custody usually wields the stick. By the time the husband gets to court to ask permission to take his son to the Super Bowl on a day when he is not ordinarily entitled to his son's custody, the special event or occasion is usually over before the matter can be heard or adjusted. Where husbands contemplate such bickering, they and their lawyers have no alternative but to attempt to perceive in advance every possible contingency and provide for them in writing.

And, unhappily, even where minutiae are covered by the

agreement, a recalcitrant wife can always cause her husband grief by claiming that the child is too ill to see the father or that he doesn't want to see the father or that he has too much homework, etc., *ad nauseam*.

Very often the suggestion is made that the custody of children be divided so that each parent has custody of one or more children. It is almost universally the rule that such a situation is to be avoided and only in rare circumstances will a court divide custody of brothers and sisters. The rule is not immutable and depends upon the ages of the children and their preferences.

Finally, we deal with the sham custody fight whereby a parent who really does not want custody does not want to admit it because he or she will look bad before the court. No wife will be given much consideration by a court where she does not want custody of her own young children. And a husband who may not want custody of his children may still ask for it simply to poison the court's mind concerning the wife and how much support she should be granted. This may become a ploy more and more in "no-fault" jurisdictions where the guilt or innocence of the parties is not deemed too crucial a matter. Thus, a husband who has the "goods on" his wife, may wish to air his knowledge and thereby influence the court, all under the guise of seeking custody.

CHAPTER 12

Sex, Sex Discrimination, and the Law

You will have noticed throughout these pages the distinctions made not only between the effects of divorce on women as opposed to men, but by the law itself both in statute and application.

It might seem to most people—and certainly to most men— that husbands emerge as the chief victims of divorce. They claim they are made to pay through the nose for their freedom from a woman they no longer love. They contend that the steady drain of alimony sharply reduces their chance to support a new wife or family, let alone live in the style to which they had been accustomed. The wife not only has the house and the money: she just sits on her duff doing nothing for the rest of her life. Why the hell can't she get a job?

Why? Because for the last five or ten or twenty years the average wife has had nothing to do but cook, clean, chauffeur, nurse, shop, and be hostess (all without pay, of course) for love of the man she married and the children she bore. And for that love, she must be a responsive sexual partner as well.

Now, many women are still content to be all these things, fulfilling what society has maintained for decades was "woman's role," and therefore, supposedly, fulfilling herself. The wife in the kitchen has been—and still is—the queen of conventional society and daytime television, and the chief target of the makers of food, detergents, domestic appliances, and cosmetics. Her *most* fulfilling role is as the nation's greatest consumer.

The working woman, on the other hand, is not. There are over forty million of them, but they don't buy as much because they have less time to shop. They still run the household in their very spare time, and, if they divorce, their husbands assume that in view of their jobs they need less support than their housebound sisters.

What many aggrieved men do not recognize is: (a) that this working wife, in whatever job, still earns far less than her male equivalent (though new laws are finally erasing this long inequity), and (b) that the housebound wife has never been trained to earn money at anything. What chance has she, then, after divorce, in a work-market demanding more and more specialized skills and accomplishments? °

° An excellent example of the law's indifference to the plight of the married woman is *Wirth* v. *Wirth*, 326 *N.Y.S.* 2d 308. One of New York's Appellate Courts stated the facts as follows: "For 22 years of marriage, the respondent delivered all his earnings to appellant, who handled the finances, to be pooled with her earnings to support the family. She paid the bills and made the investments. In 1956 he started a 'crash' savings program telling appellant it was 'for our latter days.' She says he told her it was 'for the two of us.' From then on, appellant's earnings, supplemented by rental from an upstairs apartment and part of respondent's income, were used for family expenses and respondent's remaining salary was invested. This invested money has always been respondent's. It is not property appellant transferred to him. His enrichment, it is claimed, arose because she spent her salary to meet the costs of maintaining the family, while the respondent accumulated his earnings in his own name. Appellant's argument is that she parted with her property just as surely as if she delivered her check to her husband because her earnings fulfilled his support obligations."

In denying the wife any portion of her husband's savings, the court said: "What appellant really seeks is a community property division under the guise of equitable relief. She premises her claimed right to equitable relief on the brief discussions between the parties in 1956 when respondent said he intended to save money for 'the two of them.' There was no promise or 'arrangement' born either from that incident or the parties' course of conduct thereafter. Respondent did not agree that the property would be held in joint names. (See *Hammer* v. *Hammer*, 16 Misc. 2d 749, 183 N.Y.S. 2d 754, affd. 10 A.D. 2d 557, 196 N.Y.S. 2d 596; *Craft* v. *Sanford*, 286 App. Div. 916, 142 N.Y.S. 2d 39.) The elements of concealment or misrepresentation usually found in fraudulent transactions are missing. The facts are that appellant acquiesced in the original suggestion and she has known for many years that the property was in her husband's name alone."

The male burden is largely one of his own making: the end result of aeons of male domination and female submission—willing or not. His part of the bargain of marriage was to earn the money needed to sustain home, family, and wife. Her job was to make him comfortable and rear his young.

What was wrong with that? Nothing, it seemed—until the marriage ceased to work and he or she wanted out. Unless his wife is rich, he has to support her and his family until she marries again. More often than not, she doesn't.

Since he probably does, he finds himself duly supporting two families, unless he has learned from experience that a wage-earning wife can be a blessing indeed—independent not only economically, but in a personality expressed and fulfilled.

It is a lesson he still resists. Yet in time he may recognize that the liberation of women will free him not only from part of the financial charges he is expected to assume, but from the emotional burden of a woman who has had no interests of her own except through him and their home. And though this loving dependence can be gratifying to his ego, it can also—over a period of time—become a load on his soul. Too much is expected of him, including decisions on the smallest matters as well as the large.

Conversely, the housebound wife can become the dictator simply because her need for power has no other outlet. The word "dominating" has for long been applied to the "free" woman, or career woman, along with "competitive" and "aggressive," when there is a genus of wife, domestic and home-oriented as she may be, who can in her own way reduce a man to pulp without his knowing it. In time he becomes not a man but a habit; taken for granted like the TV set. He's there, turned off more than on. Fixtures are not free.

As time goes on, it is easier to do what his wife expects of him (going to dinner with people who bore him stiff, entertaining relatives who get on his nerves, attending civic banquets) than face the familiar, exasperated face. Far easier to say "No" at the office than "No" at home.

The mask of the "good" husband can smother the inner man. The shadow of the "little woman," the full-time housewife he married, has blanked him out.

This little parable may sound exaggerated, but in it a basic core of truth exists: a husband is not free to be himself when his wife is not free to be herself—free in the sense of maintaining an inviolable identity as a human individual apart from her married role.

Women, like men, have drives and goals, one of which is the exertion of power—over human beings and circumstances. And when this drive exists in a woman who has no means to exert it outside the home, it will be directed only toward children who increasingly defy or evade it, or toward a husband who does not dare to.

The liberation of men is, therefore, a direct concomitant to (and beneficiary of) the liberation of women. Not from marriage or housework or children, if these are her desires, but from the total immersion of her faculties in a life that uses only half of them. Her male equivalent is the man who has to work and commute for ten hours a day for forty years to pay for this half, not only during marriage but after divorce.

In every real sense justice in the United States in matters of family law adds up to a marital *Rashomon*. Who is victor and who is victim, who is right and who is wrong, who is rewarded and who is punished, who is protected and who is exposed, depends on one's own personal viewpoint. Men object to being "fleeced." Women resent being on the "dole." There must be something wrong with the system. There is, as we shall see, and, contrary to widespread belief, the system is weighted heavily against women. And worse, many married women seeking divorce are paying heavily in present tribute for long-range gains they have no wish to achieve. Many courts, conscious of the Woman's Liberation Movement, are applying new "liberal" concepts to women who don't want to be liberated now and who never asked to be when they were married.

Since 1868, the Constitution of the United States has provided that ". . . No state shall make or enforce any law which shall abridge the privileges or immunities of citizens of the United States . . . nor deny to any person within its jurisdiction the equal protection of the laws."

Only once in its history has the Supreme Court of the United States invalidated a state statute on the ground that it denied to women (or men) the equal protection of the laws within the meaning of the Fourteenth Amendment. In November 1971 the U.S. Supreme Court held that an Idaho law preferring men over women in the administration of estates, when the purpose of the law was simply to avoid the necessity of a hearing to determine who was better qualified to serve as administrator, violated the Fourteenth Amendment. The court said, unanimously, that "to give a mandatory preference to members of either sex over members of the other merely to accomplish the elimination of hearings . . . is to make the very kind of arbitrary legislative choice forbidden by the equal protection clause." In other words, the court has held that state statutes that permit sex discrimination are invalid where there is no sound reason for the discrimination permitted.

But the court has not overruled *Goesaert* v. *Cleary*, 335 U.S. 464 (1948), which constitutes its latest decision on the subject of sex discrimination in state statutes prior to its consideration of the Idaho statute. The *Goesaert* case involved a Michigan statute that forbade the licensing of female bartenders unless she be "the wife or daughter of the male owner" of a licensed bar. In upholding the statute against a claim that it treated women differently than men, in contravention of the Constitution, Judge Frankfurter said:

The fact that women may now have achieved the virtues that men have long claimed as their prerogatives and now indulge in vices that men have long practiced, does not preclude the States from drawing a sharp line between the sexes, certainly in such matters as the regulation of the liquor traffic. . . . The Constitution does not require legislatures to reflect sociological insight, or shifting social standards, any more than it requires them to keep abreast of the latest scientific standards.

Although the decision of the Supreme Court, involving the Idaho statute, at first blush seems to give heart to the hopes of many lawyers that our courts will now scrutinize sex-based discriminatory statutes, and although many state statutes will face new legal battles before courts which will be more sympathetic to the argument that the statutes are unconstitutional, it is still true that where a "reasonable" reason is given by the various state legislatures for discriminating against one sex and in favor of the other, the statutes will be upheld. Our courts seem to have read into the Fourteenth Amendment, insofar as discrimination in favor of one sex or the other is concerned, an exception which has not been found when applying the Fourteenth Amendment to cases based upon discrimination in favor of one race against others.

Women have been discriminated for and against by state statutes in a variety of fields such as employment opportunities, property ownership, use of their own name, choice of their own domicile, criminal responsibility, rights to sue for the loss of love, affection, companionship, society and sexual relations of their spouses, grounds of divorce, even the use of profanity, and many many others since this nation's inception.°

The historical roots of such discrimination run deep and are reflective of the original legal notions of "coverture." This historical background has been succinctly stated recently, as follows:

° Excellent articles on the subject of sex discrimination among the states have been written. Among these are: Sex-Based Discrimination in American Law. II. Law and the Married Woman, Kanowitz 12 *St. Louis University Law Journal* 3–73; The Equal Rights Amendment; a Constitutional Basis for Equal Rights for Women; 80 *Yale Law Journal* 872–985 (April 1971); Sex Discrimination and Equal Protection; Do We Need a Constitutional Amendment? 84 *Harvard Law Review* 1499–1524 (April 1971); Amending the Constitution to Prohibit State Discrimination Based on Sex, 26 Record of New York City Bar Association 77–90 (1971); Sexual Problems and Marital Dissolution. Robert Veit Sherwin, *Medical Aspects of Human Sexuality*, Vol. IV, No. 4 (April 1970).

At common law, a woman who married became a legal non-person—a *femme couverte*. Upon marriage, she lost virtually all legal status as an individual human being and was regarded by the law almost entirely in terms of her relationship with her husband. Statutory developments in the nineteenth and early twentieth centuries tended to frame a more dignified but nevertheless distinct and circumscribed legal status for married women. At the present time domestic relations law is based on a network of legal disabilities for women, supposedly compensated by a corresponding network of legal protections. The law in this area treats women, by turns, as mental incompetents and as more mature persons than men of the same age; as valuable domestic servants of their husbands and as economic incompetents; as needing protection from their husbands' economic selfishness and as needing no protection from their husbands' physical abusiveness. In many respects, such as name and domicile, the law continues overtly to subordinate a woman's identity to her husband's.°

Although the status of women has come a long way in the direction of dignity and equality, it still has a long way to go. Many attempts have been made to convince the Congress, state legislatures, and courts that men and women should be treated equally. Even today legal scholars cannot agree on how to attack the problem. The New York City Bar Association, for example, in its recent report rejected a constitutional amendment to provide for such equality of treatment and recommended federal legislation "drawn as far as possible to deal with specific subject matter, and a continuing pattern of judicial decision under the Equal Protection Clause of the Fourteenth Amendment." Other writers scoff at the slim progress made by our courts in this field and consider federal legislation too piecemeal and too uncertain to grant equality or to convince state courts to grant it with the required dispatch.

Although an equal rights amendment was passed overwhelmingly in the House of Representatives during the Ninety-first

° 80 *Yale Law Journal* 937 (April 1971).

Congress in 1970, final passage in the Senate was blocked and whether such an amendment will pass in the near future and how it would affect woman's equality remains problematical. This is perhaps truer now with a more "strict constructionist" Supreme Court than it has been in the past decade.

In the field of domestic relations, permissible sex discrimination among the states abounds. For example, in most states, married women have no right to the free choice of their domicile. In most states a woman must assume her husband's name and in some she must retain that name even after divorce. In some states, wives are not entitled to any portion of their husband's capital assets, regardless of the wife's contribution in terms of services and help in amassing them. In the eight community-property states, Arizona, California, Idaho, Louisiana, Nevada, New Mexico, Texas, and Washington, property not acquired by gift or as a legacy from an estate, is owned during the marriage by both husband and wife. The husband usually has the power of management over the community property and in some states he can transfer it without his wife's consent. Some states even grant to a husband but not to his spouse, a defense in a homicide case where the wife, at the time of the homicide, was having sexual intercourse with another person. And, of course, there are discriminatory laws concerning the question of custody and concerning different grounds for divorce. The Kentucky statute, for example, (Baldwin's Kentucky Revised Statutes 403.020) in an exceptional case of male chauvinism provides in part as follows:

(3) A divorce may be granted to the wife for the following causes:

(a) When not in like fault, habitual drunkenness on the part of the husband of not less than one year's duration, accompanied by a wasting of the husband's estate and without any suitable provision for the maintenance of the wife or children;

(b) Habitually behaving toward her, for not less than six months in such cruel and inhuman manner as to indicate a settled aversion to her or to destroy permanently her peace or happiness; or

(c) Such cruel beating or injury, or attempt at injury, of the wife as indicates an outrageous temper in the husband, or probable danger to her life, or of great bodily injury, from her remaining with him. (1962 c 210, §49. Eff. 6–14–62. 1956 c 72; 1950 c 162; 1956 c 74)

(4) A divorce may be granted to the husband for the following causes:

(a) Where the wife is pregnant by another man without the husband's knowledge at the time of marriage;

(b) When not in like fault, habitual drunkenness on the part of the wife of not less than one year's duration;

(c) Adultery by the wife, or such lewd, lascivious behavior on her part as proves her to be unchaste, without actual proof of an act of adultery;

(d) Habitually behaving toward him, for not less than six months in such cruel and inhuman manner as to indicate a settled aversion to him or to destroy permanently his peace or happiness; or

(e) Such cruel beating or injury, or attempt at injury, of the husband as indicates an outrageous temper in the wife, or probable danger to his life or great bodily injury, from his remaining with her.*

And do not statutes such as New York's, which bar alimony to a wife guilty of adultery or guilty of abandonment or such cruel and inhuman treatment as would entitle her husband to a divorce, involve similar discrimination? A husband suffers no economic penalty in New York if he commits adultery, even if it was his conduct to begin with which sparked his wife's misconduct. It is even so if his adultery was open, continuous, and reprehensible, although his wife's may be entirely justifiable in the opinion of any impartial lawyer, psychiatrist, or sociologist. Of course, the New York statute could achieve the same result if

---

* The same statute further provides that either party may receive a divorce if the other is "living in adultery."

the law provided, as it does in other states, that in appropriate circumstances, a husband could receive support from his wife. Although such a statute would achieve legal equality, its application would still be onerous to dependent wives committing excusable adultery. Florida, as we shall see, permits the court, but does not direct it, to consider adultery in determining the amount of alimony.

It is not that the law is making no strides toward achieving sensible and workable divorce laws. The decisions and statutes, however, are fragmented and at times irreconcilable, and change is coming slowly, indeed. The U.S. Supreme Court has at least recognized a new concept of privacy. It has stricken, for example, a Connecticut statute making the sale of contraceptives to married couples illegal (*Griswold* v. *Connecticut*, 381 U.S. 479 [1965]).

Many state statutes are being repealed so that married men and women, wishing to engage in some of the intimacies urged by marriage manuals, may no longer be committing crimes as they still are in several states. Those manuals, for example, frequently urge couples to engage in any form of sexual behavior such as oral genital stimulation, provided each of the parties enjoys that sort of thing.

It is no doubt true that every great crusade must sacrifice as victims some of the people it intended to benefit. Unfortunately (and unwittingly), this has been the unforeseen result of liberal divorce laws as they are being applied to those people who never asked for them when they were married.

As more and more states adopt and accept a new sociological concept of divorce, the courts are applying this divorce ideology to broken marriages between men and women to whom such new ideas are wholly or partially inapplicable.

It is one thing to recognize that spouses should be able to separate or divorce when their marriages have "broken down" or where there are "irreconcilable differences" or where the parties have been living apart voluntarily or by court decree for a period of time. This motion does little violence to the continued happiness and well-being of partners to "dead marriages." But it is quite another thing to apply to older marriages new and unfair standards and criteria—however innovative—of measuring how much support to award the wife for herself and her children.

It is now frequently argued and accepted as a matter of state law that women should be encouraged to work, to avoid indolence, to accept training for jobs, to become useful and independent of their spouses—very good for marriages entered into in that spirit. Fine dogma for the new marriages between the young who regard marriage more and more as an equal partnership. But it is sheer nonsense to apply such relatively "new" standards to couples married before the birth or, at least, the maturation of such concepts.

Women's liberation, no matter how widely reported, is still no doubt rejected by far more people (including women) than those who accept it. And it has barely even been recognized by our courts, which have time and again upheld laws which discriminate against women and which historically and presently treat women as more suited for domesticity than as equals to men with the same rights, privileges, and abilities.

The vast majority of women never entered an economically equal partnership or did they intend to. Many understood that marriage with childbirth might terminate their working careers, that their husbands would provide for them and the children, and that they could put away their working skills in favor of adopting more "domestic" ones. Many a woman with scholastic honors and many others with bright career futures sacrificed them and their personal freedom to the home and children.

These same women are now told that a new day has come. They are instructed that while the duration of the marriage is important and the number of children they have borne is relevant in determining support, other factors, of which they were never apprised before, are also "relevant." In New York, for example, they learn that they have no right to share in their husband's assets or "to become his partner" even as to his income.

They are instructed that where the children have grown and left the house, they should train for work, and then go out and find employment to ease the husband's burden.

But in marriages past, what of the woman who for the love of husband and children (even, if misguided) gave all her dedication to the family? What of the countless wives who worked to put their husbands through school, who worked until their husbands asked them to stay home and take care of the children? And what happens to those, even, who sacrificed their earning potential with the assent and cooperation—possibly at the insistence—of the husband?

Is it not grievously unfair to direct a forty-five-year-old woman whose children are now full grown, to enter, after a quarter of a century, an unskilled labor market or to train to do so, unless it is essential to support a divorce? Is it not manifestly unjust to proclaim that a marriage which progressed by the joint efforts of man and wife to a point where the husband has acquired sufficient assets, income, and station in life, to share these with his partner is less than a full partnership regardless of our "new insight" that even older marriages may die or become useless? Is it not obvious that where "grounds" or "fault" should play little or no part in determining whether there should be a divorce, that the history of the relationship should be profoundly important in determining the manner and style by which the wife and children shall be supported? Some courts have the flexibility required to do what is just between man and wife. The new "no-fault" divorce bill adopted in Florida, for example, provides as follows (Florida Statutes, Section 61,08):

(1) In a proceeding for dissolution of marriage, the court may grant alimony to either party, which alimony may be rehabilitative or permanent in nature. In any award of alimony the court may order periodic payments or payments in lump sum or both. The court may consider the adultery of a spouse and the circumstances thereof in determining whether alimony shall be awarded to such spouse and the amount of alimony, if any, to be awarded to such spouse.

(2) In determining a proper award of alimony, the court may consider any factor necessary to do equity and justice between the parties.

But few states have articulated or accepted into the fabric of their law the notion that marriage for many women is an institution by which they become emotional and economical cripples in one way or another. Where this happens, women have not become so solely by their own actions, but often with the help, acquiescence, and approval of the husband. Where this occurs, the woman's dependent economic status should be recognized and, where practical, given full consideration.

In many states the governing statutes and decisions seem to lose sight of the impossibility of applying certain criteria to certain marriages.

New York State, for example (Domestic Relations Law, Section 236) enables the court to "direct the husband to provide suitably for the support of the wife as, in the court's discretion, justice requires, for a regard to the length of time of the marriage, the ability of the wife to be self-supporting, the circumstances of the case and of those respective parties. . . ."

The statute has been applied harshly—with strong emphasis upon the wife's own resources, upon her ability to work, and upon the necessity of her remaining home with young children. In New York a wife is not to be considered a husband's partner in terms of his capital assets. Why not, if that is what the parties intended? Why not, if the parties elected to lead their lives in such a way that the husband was the aggressive provider and the wife the domestic appendage?

Many working wives have led marital lives of long duration and maintained their own identities, their own careers, their own bank accounts, and their own securities and other assets. Many couples with marriages of long duration have never regarded their economic relationship as being joint or equal. The standard for them should not be the same as for couples who agreed to follow the "husband-is-the-breadwinner doctrine." The New York statute would be far more equitable as would the de-

cisions under it, if it were left to the sound discretion of the
court to do justice between the parties in the light of their marital expectations, their marital history, and their own particular
economic realities, as they developed during the course of the
marriage.

Every matrimonial lawyer has represented women who have
genuinely gone into shock upon learning that what they regarded as "theirs" turned out to be "his." In too many states this
inequity persists, not only when the wife stayed at home but
when she worked in order to help support the family and discovered that this help enabled her husband to salt away funds
in his own name because he was able to save by reason of her
labors.°

We do not opt for rules of law which encourage marital dependence. We have little hope for marriages contracted or fulfilled through female economic obeisance. But we do recognize
that most marriages of long duration are already infected by the
present reality of male economic superiority, that the wife very
often abandons commercial productivity in favor of domestic
productivity (or nonproductivity), and that in the near future
this trend will not be sharply reversed. No compelling interest
of the state demands that the law should not be flexible enough
to make allowance for marital unions where the wife and husband jointly agree that the wife remains in the home. There is
no reason why the state should adopt laws punitive to such an
arrangement.

Perhaps part of the judicial antipathy shown toward women
by male-dominated courts arises because of the many hundreds

° To be contrasted with our views, however, is the view of one of New
York's Appellate Courts in *Phillips* v. *Phillips*, 1 A. D. 2d 393, 396, affd. 2
New York 2d 742, that women have "practically unlimited opportunities . . .
in the business world of today." In the same case the court said that, "in an
era where the opportunities for self-support by the wife are so abundant the
fact that the marriage has been brought to an end because of the fault of
the husband does not necessarily entitle the wife to be forever supported
by a former husband who has little, if any, more economic advantage than
she has." These views were only recently restated and approved by New
York's highest court in *Kover* v. *Kover*, New York 2d (1972).

of cases heard each year where women on legal advice attempt to overreach and continue economically outrageous existences far beyond the ability of their husbands to provide. Such instances surely must sour courts in applying alimony statutes. But because we live in a male-dominated society and are governed by male-dominated legislatures and courts, it must be remembered that husbands who are willing to pay too little are merely called "penurious" or "penny pinchers" or "tightwads," while their counterparts are called "ball-breakers," "bitches," "c—ts," and worse.

The decision between a man and a woman concerning who should get what is a delicate one and of enormous concern only to the single family unit involved. The factors which must be considered in rendering an equitable division of assets are many, and the process of weighing such factors is tremendously time-consuming. Nevertheless, thousands of men and women each year find themselves facing bleak futures because the judicial process failed one or the other of the parties in their quest for equity.

CHAPTER 13

Of Adultery and Private Investigators

On the night of February 17, 1963, a lucky man named Pierre registered at a hotel in Westchester County using his own name. Shortly thereafter the Defendant Wife was proven to have entered and examined the room that had been assigned to Pierre. Not liking the room, she had another one substituted for him. The Defendant Wife stayed in this room, and early in the morning of February 18 she was seen through a partially open door in a "shortie" night gown.

It was further proven that Pierre attended a small party in the hotel's bar while the Defendant Wife called several times seeking his whereabouts. At 4 o'clock in the morning of February 18, Pierre was discovered, not in the room of the Defendant Wife, but in that of another woman. The Plaintiff Husband was denied a divorce on the grounds of adultery.

In another case in the same state, New York, it was proven that the Defendant Wife, while separated from her husband, had made "frequent expressions of attachment" for her alleged lover; that they had made many social appearances together; that the Defendant Wife had been taking contraceptive pills while living in the alleged paramour's one-family household for four months. New York's highest court affirmed orders of the lower courts dismissing the complaint, in an action for a divorce on the ground of adultery.

In yet another New York case, the Defendant Husband met his alleged paramour at a railroad station, took her to a hotel, where he registered himself and his lover under an assumed name as husband and wife. After a room had been assigned to the couple they went into the elevator, the Defendant Husband carrying the baggage. Neither he nor his paramour were seen to have come downstairs again at least up to midnight. A New York court, granting a divorce, said: "We have it of old that 'it is presumed he saith not a pater noster' there."

In New York "the mere fact" that a man and woman live alone together is not in itself sufficient evidence of adultery. Nor is it sufficient to prove adultery that a defendant sometimes ate meals and occasionally remained overnight, without further proof of intimacy. It has been held in New York that even the fact that the Defendant and an alleged lover went on a boat trip together and had adjoining rooms at a hotel would not prove adultery.

One could describe interminably the infinitely varied circumstances under which husbands and wives attempt to prove and disprove the commission of adultery. We have already explained that there are some few states which have adopted genuine no-fault divorce statutes in which adultery is either supposed to be wholly irrelevant, or at least relevant only with respect to the question of support for the wife and children.

But the question of whether or not an act of adultery has taken place, except theoretically, is of great legal moment in the vast majority of states; and on a pragmatic basis it is extremely material and important in every state. It bears on questions of custody and the amount of support, and weighs heavily on the conscience of the court and the couples. In those states where the court is given great latitude in dividing the marital assets, the husband may be as much affected as the wife. And even in those states where no such discretion exists, a husband guilty of adultery under circumstances that offend the court's conscience may well be required, regardless of the applicable state law, to pay more support for the wife and children than if his conduct were "unblemished."

Unfortunately, the overwhelming majority of courts see the question of adultery as a clear-cut proposition. Either he did or he didn't, or she did or she didn't. Why he did or why she did seems never to be the issue, although to us it seems to be the only issue. Adultery is the isolated commission, by husband or wife, of an act of sexual intercourse with a third person. Only recently in New York has that included an act of homosexuality. Not only does adultery cover long-term, deliberate, and destructive affairs—committed by one partner or another with total disregard for the feelings of the mate and the welfare of the children—but it also includes isolated acts of "infidelity" committed by the distraught, the mentally unstable, the temporarily anguished, the drunk and the drugged, the victim and the victimizer.

In this particular area, and in the light of all we know of the pressures of marriage and the frailties of human beings, it is senseless to punish the so-called guilty without regard to the background against which the alleged transgression occurred. The question should not be: Did he or she commit adultery, but *Why* did he or she commit adultery? Laws which dissolve marriages, deny wives support or distribution of property, or punish husbands simply because an act of adultery has taken place without regard to the surrounding circumstances are anachronisms flung in the face of reality.

In New York, as in many other states, the true mental condition of the adulterer or adulteress constitutes no defense to a divorce action based upon adultery unless he or she is actually and legally "incompetent and irresponsible for the acts charged."

In one case the wife, having admitted to committing adultery, interposed a defense that at the time of the alleged act she was mentally and emotionally incompetent and irresponsible.

At first the court pondered whether it should apply the an-

cient criminal rule, still viable in many states, that affords as a
defense to criminal acts the inability of the defendant "to distinguish right from wrong or to understand the nature and quality
of the act."

The court suggested that another alternative would be to determine whether the wife was suffering from a mental disease, of
which the adultery in question was the result, and which she
would not have committed if she were stable. It also considered
applying a rule that no penalty should be imposed "upon one
who is a victim of conditions beyond her control, and not a willing, rational actor." The court decided, in granting a divorce to
the husband, that it need not make a choice and stated its reasons as follows:

> The burden of proving mental condition relieving defendant
> of responsibility is on defendant (*Laudo* v. *Laudo*, 188 App.
> Div. 699, 706 supra; see, also, *Matter of Jacobs*, 2 A.D. 2d.
> 774, affd. 3 N.Y. 2d 723). Her sanity is presumed and the pre-
> sumption must be overcome by a contrary showing (*Matter of
> Jacobs*, supra). To overcome the presumption, defendant of-
> fered the testimony of her psychiatrist and the record of her
> hospitalization at Meadowbrook a few days after the incident
> which is the basis of this action. The psychiatrist testified that
> defendant had been under his care since September, 1960;
> that she was even now highly unstable; that he had first diag-
> nosed her condition as a character disorder, but later con-
> cluded that she was schizophrenic-affective type; that when
> hospitalized at Meadowbrook she was quite irrational and
> talking of destroying herself, but that he felt that committing
> her to Pilgrim State would destroy her ability for re-integra-
> tion and, therefore, took her back as a private case; that in his
> opinion it was best for her to be working and that she, there-
> fore, has been attending Speedwriting classes since shortly
> after she left Meadowbrook Hospital. After the incident, the
> psychiatrist testified that he had asked her indirectly if she
> had committed adultery since and she had evaded the ques-
> tion; that prior to the incident, she was aware that she was
> being followed since plaintiff had told her in the presence of

the psychiatrist that as a result of previous infidelities he intended to have her followed; that defendant had discussed the rendezvous with the witness three days before it occurred and told him that she had sought to dissuade her paramour from going through with it and had told the paramour that he might be involved in a lawsuit; that defendant nonetheless felt compelled to go ahead with the meeting; that she was motivated by emotionality rather than rational thinking and felt justified in what she was going to do; that she was unable to determine that it was a wrong act; that it was for her primarily a means of getting even with her father, and to a lesser degree with plaintiff, both of whom considered her a "bad" person; that in his opinion she was unable to control her actions and in poor contact with reality at the time of the incident, and was then unable to distinguish the true nature of the act she was committing or to differentiate right from wrong; that although she knew vaguely that what she was doing was contrary to law and social conventions, she was not aware of the legal or social consequences; that when she had sufficient health, she would not engage in extra-marital relations and because she got as far into the act as plaintiff's proof of the incident showed, he concluded that she was no longer capable of making a decision concerning it. The hospital record shows an initial impression of schizophrenic reaction, affective type, chronic, severe, but this was changed a few days later to character disorder. There is a notation that "she is quite aggressive sexually" and the nurse's notes of January 28, 1962, detail incidents in the ward, which, apparently, form the basis for that conclusion, including overtures of a homosexual nature.

On the other side of the scale is the testimony of plaintiff's psychiatrist that in his opinion, while defendant has had psychiatric difficulty and was emotionally unstable and in need of treatment, she was sufficiently intact to be able to use the ordinary standards of right and wrong; that she behaved in a manner which indicated that she was aware of those factors; that she knew at the time of the incident that she was committing adultery and that it was wrong; that she is not schizophrenic, and that her stating to him that she had no recollection of the incident but was able quickly and accurately to supply data unrelated to the incident, indicated to him that she was lying in an attempt to evade discussion of the incident with him. Also to be weighed are (1) the testimony of two investigators, members of the raiding party, that when they broke into the hotel room defendant jumped up from bed, cried out "Oh, no" repeatedly and ran toward the bathroom, (2) the photograph of defendant standing completely nude near the bathroom door, her face covered by a towel, (3) defendant's affidavit of February 26, 1962, which recounts in detail and with coherence her problems with her parents and with plaintiff and plaintiff's finances, and among other things states that as a result of an hysterectomy "I felt the need for proving myself as a woman. I had to be assured that I was still wanted as a woman," (4) defendant's failure, though present in the courthouse, to testify or even to enter the courtroom where the trial was being held.

The court concludes that defendant has not sustained the burden of proof. Had she testified, the impressions gained by the court during her testimony would have supported the opinion of one or the other of the psychiatrists. At the base of the differing opinions of the experts is their differing views of her credibility. Her credibility is also the central issue in this case. Deprived of the opportunity of forming first-hand impressions concerning defendant's credibility, the court can choose between the experts' views only on the basis of the consistency of those views with the evidence as a whole. The inconsistency between the conclusion that defendant was driven into acts of adultery by an irrational necessity to get even with her father and with plaintiff and, on the one hand the homosexual overtures at the hospital, and, on the other, the implication in defendant's affidavit that the acts of adultery resulted from the necessity of proving herself a woman, suggests to the court that the hospital overtures and the affidavit's contention are afterthoughts contrived by defendant to escape the consequences of her act. That defendant went ahead with her tryst notwithstanding she had been warned she was being followed, can be interpreted as irrational, but might also indicate either disbelief that plaintiff would take action, or a rational conclusion on her part that her relationship with plaintiff had so far deteriorated that she did not care whether the marriage continued or not. While her statement to her psychiatrist that she tried to talk the paramour out of going ahead with their plans is consistent with irrationality, her actions when caught and thereafter, as demonstrated by word and deed, suggest a realization of the nature of her conduct and a desire to avoid its consequences. On all of the evidence the court concludes that defendant has not demonstrated by a preponderance of the credible evidence that she was, as pleaded in her separate defense, "suffering from mental and emotional disorders so as to make her incompetent and irresponsible for the acts charged against her in the complaint."

We again caution that each state has its individual rules concerning what proof is required to establish adultery and what defenses are available. In many states, for example, the defenses of recrimination or "comparative rectitude" are available; and an action for divorce based on adultery may be defended if it is shown that the plaintiff is also guilty of such conduct. In some states the comparative "fault" is weighed. In many states condonation or forgiveness is a defense. In other states various statutes of limitations can serve as a defense. In New York, an act of adultery committed more than five years before a divorce action may not be the basis for a divorce action.

Generally, proof of an adulterous act must be reasonably convincing, and the court must not be left with a mere suspicion that the act took place.

It is obvious, however, that adultery is usually not conducted in the open, and that those committing it are as clandestine as possible. Many courts have adopted a rule, such as that in New York, that in order to establish that adultery has taken place, plaintiff must prove opportunity, inclination, *and* intent. It is not enough to show any single element; all must be present. The fact that the defendant entered into an invalid subsequent marriage has been held to be insufficient evidence of adultery without further proof of residence with the new spouse. The fact that the defendant may have spent hours alone with an alleged lover and had all the opportunity in the world to commit adultery is of itself insufficient.

There are special rules relating to the admissibility of various kinds of evidence to prove adultery. They deal with the confessions of spouses and lovers, with letters and other communications between husbands and wives, with the amount of weight different kinds of proof should be accorded which, in turn, may depend upon who is testifying. As a matter of public policy for example, and in order to prevent collusive divorces, adultery may not be proven on the testimony of the defendant alone. Generally, it is insufficient to base a decree granting a divorce solely on the statements of a paramour whose testimony is regarded with suspicion.

Lawyers who want to research the law on any given subject consult what are known as state law digests. If, for example, a lawyer wanted to examine a question involving fraud and misrepresentation concerning contracts, he would consult the relevant digest under the general heading "Contracts," finding under that general heading another general subheading "Fraud and Misrepresentation." That subheading might lead in turn to "materiality of representation," "intent to deceive," "reliance on representation," "representations as to future events," and so forth.

A lawyer who wanted to research the amount of weight to be given to a private detective's testimony in a divorce action would consult the law digest under the general heading "Divorce." Under that heading he would find a subheading called '-'adultery" and (as in New York), a further subheading entitled "testimony of prostitutes, detectives or persons of low character." And although many "low characters" are responsible for the conviction of others for the most serious crimes, and although many a sad husband or wife has been found to have committed adultery by evidence produced by such "low characters," it is still true that their testimony is regarded with great suspicion by the law.

Our courts recognize that detectives or "private investigators," which is what the state prefers to call them, are hired mercenaries whose reputation and economic well-being depend upon producing "the goods." In fairness, however, we doubt that the historical lumping together of all detectives with prostitutes and others of dubious character is either accurate or fair. There are good private investigators and bad ones; there are reliable ones and unreliable ones. Some are honest, some questionable. Some are capable and some are disastrous bunglers. And if one were to distinguish further between private detectives and prostitutes, it should be clear that the former deliver the goods far more seldom than do the latter.

Everybody dislikes the idea of being spied upon. But since the law places such great importance upon that old devil "adultery," and husbands and wives so often concoct such mischievous and falsified pictures of their finances, and divorce proceedings are still held largely on an advocacy basis with the party holding the best hand emerging the "winner," the use of spies will continue.

It is usually the wife who needs the services of a private detective most: she must, in many states, prove "fault" before she is entitled to support; very often she cannot afford the services of an investigator. The wife whose husband has buried his assets and hidden his sources of income is often unable to pay for them. The wife who, in a custody case, would need investigators, psychiatrists, psychologists, and other experts, frequently finds that their very expensive talents are available to her husband, but not to her.

It is, of course, quite true that where the husband "catches" his wife committing adultery, or proves that she is guilty of other grounds for divorce, he may reap a real windfall and be excused totally or partially from the responsibility of supporting the wife. And in the many, many states where this is true, a wife "caught in the act" is in a far worse position than her husband, who suffers either no financial penalty or very little, depending upon the jurisdiction and the particular morals of the judge or jury.

Those husbands and wives of modest means must rely upon their lawyers and their friends to come up with the necessary evidence, while the more fortunate can avail themselves of the often crucial knowledge, experience, and inventiveness of a private investigator.

The private investigator in New York is subject to several regulations found in the State's General Business Law. They are required to be licensed. They are forbidden to accept employment in whole or in part on a contingent or percentage basis. Their backgrounds are investigated, and they may not employ persons who have been convicted of certain crimes. A licensed detective must post a surety bond and must have served an apprenticeship for a period of not less than three years. And in addition to being vulnerable to the loss of his license, he may be subject to various reprisals by employers who have sustained damages as a result of his misconduct or that of his employees.

The following cases illustrate the ingenuity that a private detective might demonstrate:

LAWYER: I want to find out whether a certain Hollywood starlet, now living in New York with her brother and sister-in-law, is pregnant. She is supposed to be the sweetheart of X, a Hollywood actor.

DETECTIVE (*after getting the relevant information and names and after about a week has gone by*): We either have to get some undiluted urine from the lady, which is impossible, or we have to get some of her blood. In order to do that we have to hire a bloodmobile to go out into the suburbs on the block where this lady lives and solicit blood from her and her neighbors. We will need a doctor and, even if we could do it, it would cost over $15,000.

LAWYER: And your license, my license, and the doctor's license.

DETECTIVE: I hadn't thought about your license or the doctor's license.

LAWYER: Find another way.

DETECTIVE (*one week later*): She isn't pregnant.

LAWYER: How do you know?

DETECTIVE: Well I figured that since this woman was from California she would use her sister-in-law's gynecologist, so I had one of our women operatives call up the sister-in-law, hysterically saying that she has just moved into the block, that she was bleeding all over the place, and that she needed a gynecologist. The sister-in-law was very nice and gave my operative the name of her gynecologist.

We looked him up and found that he was associated with the XYZ Hospital. I found out that the hospital administrator was named Dr. Jones. I then called the doctor that was recommended to my operative and told him that I was Dr. Jones, that the hospital had just been sued for malpractice, and that he too was named as a defendant.

The gynecologist asked me what he was supposed to have done wrong and I told him that he was charged with giving X-ray treatments to the woman we were interested in while she was pregnant.

We were really lucky since the doctor knew the woman and sure enough he had treated her, but not for a pregnancy. He said that he had treated her for a very minor gynecological problem and he positively stated that the woman wasn't pregnant.

Another Scene

LAWYER: I represent a woman whose husband has earned $100,000 per year and he suddenly claims that he has been fired and that he is broke. My client doesn't believe him, but his boss, who has been his friend for years, claims that the husband has indeed been fired.

DETECTIVE (*three weeks later*): Your client is right, the husband is full of shit. This guy has a great reputation as a garment salesman in New York. I have a friend in the midwest whose buddy works for a large garment manufacturer in Wisconsin.

I spent a lot of time getting the dope on this company, and "borrowing" the letterhead of the midwestern company, I wrote hubby telling him that Mr. Smith, from "our company," would be in New York in ten days and would like to talk to him confidentially.

I contacted the son-of-a-bitch and we spent the night drinking last night. I told him about how anxious we are to set up a New York subsidiary and I gave him a lot of crap about stock options and he could name his own price. When he told me that he was making $100,000 a year, I told him that I thought that was a little steep, but if he was the right man, we could still substantially better the offer.

About one-thirty in the morning, when we were talking about how unhappy I was with my own marriage, I told him that we had heard a rumor that he was about to be fired, so the son-of-a-bitch then says: "Well, as a matter of fact, I am technically not working for the company any more."

He then did about forty minutes about his troubles with your client and what a bitch she is and he told me that he was "off the books" until he settles with your client.

I then told him "Boy you must have some smart lawyer." He just winked; then he had the nerve to spend another half hour trying to repair my marriage.

The hiring of detectives is very costly. The average rate in New York City is $150 a day for an eight-hour day for two investigators, plus their expenses such as phone calls, gas, meals, etc. Although the detective is recommended by the lawyer, financial arrangements are usually made directly between the detective and the client, and the detective almost always insists upon being paid well in advance by the client. They realize the pitfalls of not getting their money in advance, and are never willing to count on the satisfaction of the client.

Two detectives are required in cases involving the investigation of matrimonial misconduct for a number of reasons. It is simply too easy to lose people being shadowed in busy cities such as New York if a detective has to worry about parking a car or retrieving it when he needs it. Many buildings and hotels have more than one entrance and somebody always has to be on the job when one or the other of the detectives wants to eat, go to the men's room, talk to a hotel clerk, garage attendant, etc. And, indeed, no job lasting more than a few days and being worked by reputable detectives comes off so smoothly that, even with two men working, some day isn't wasted because the party being "tailed" loses his followers in traffic or turns out to be the wrong person, or because of some other mishap. It is a rare detective who can report truthfully the whereabouts of the person he is following every hour of every day. This is usually not because the person being followed is cautious but simply due to the inherent difficulties of trailing people in large cities.

The wisdom, necessity, and extent of utilizing detectives depends upon the circumstances. It doesn't always work, and might backfire. The client's major risks are that the investment may not pay off and that far from proving that the suspected spouse is doing something wrong, hiring detectives may prove that he or she is innocent or too smart to get caught. Where the party who is followed knows about it and behaves himself long enough to reach trial, it is a damaging piece of evidence for the opposing lawyer to be able to point out that his client can't afford squandering money on detectives and to postulate further how much a victim his client is, married to such a suspicious mate who needed private detectives to prove that his client was innocent of all wrongdoing.

LAWYER: It is humiliating and disgraceful, Your Honor, this woman goes out and hires detectives when neither she nor my client can afford it. We have subpoenaed the reports rendered by the detective agency, and all that has been proven is that my client is not only not an adulterer, but that he is married to a woman whose suspicions throughout their marriage have mutilated the relationship. . . .

While the evidence collected by private detectives may serve to confirm or disprove marital suspicion and have an important psychological influence on a client, a good deal of evidence must be collected before the court will accept it as proof of adultery. The inclination of most clients and many attorneys is to stop too soon once the detective has uncovered evidence of infidelity sufficient to prove it to the client. The latter often makes the disastrous judgment that the same amount of evidence will convince the court or a jury in those states where jury trials are permitted. Most husbands think that all they need to know is that their wives had lunch twice last week with a certain man; that she held hands with the man, kissed him several times in the taxi cab, and spent two hours alone with him in a hotel room, to assume to their own satisfaction that the wife is "playing around." Such evidence may not be convincing at all to a court.

The wife's story may be that the man was an old friend who, she foolishly believed, would give her a job—even though she can't type or handle a switchboard. He wasn't kissing her in the cab but whispering to her that she was being followed. She went to the man's hotel because he told her that he wanted her to meet his secretary. The ensuing two hours were spent trying to convince the man that even though she was being divorced from her husband, she still loved him very much. It is true that when she went downstairs she kissed the man good-by, but what the detective didn't hear her say was, "Conrad, we have been very good friends for many years, let's keep it that way."

It depends upon how sympathetic a particular judge or jury is. What seems, at first, to be a "cinch case" often turns out to be a loser when a sympathetic court or jury finds that not enough opportunity, inclination, or intent has been established. Where there is room for doubt there is room for discretion, and judges and juries are often far more lenient in the application of evidence to rules of law that they think too harsh in a given case. When a client can evoke enough sympathy to cause the judge or jury to believe that an indiscretion was justified, it is too simple to find that the indiscretion did not take place, or that the excuse for it, however bizarre, was proven, and to refuse to give credence to the testimony of paid witnesses such as detectives.

Lawyers, also, are interested in keeping expenses down in matrimonial cases, not only for the benefit of the client, but because the total family budget cannot provide for large expenses for investigations and high counsel fees. Often they, too, terminate the investigation before there is sufficient evidence.

Sometimes, of course, very little evidence is needed—simply because of the embarrassment felt by one spouse in being caught. Where the husband has been seeing the wife's best friend or the wife has been indiscreet with the husband's boss, there is no need to go further by getting additional evidence because the party who is "caught" is embarrassed to the point where he or she agrees to settle out of a sense of humiliation.

As the law imposes an obligation to prove fault in most states and imposes strict rules of evidence in proving it, it often becomes necessary to satisfy the law's requirements and to thwart the possibility of coming up against a sympathetic judge or jury to "pull the raid." A matrimonial raid consists, usually, of at least two detectives, a photographer (who should be a professional and who should be able to take pictures accurately while ducking several punches from enraged lovers and other combatants), the angered spouse, and perhaps a relative or friend.°

Most detectives deny that they engage in matrimonial raids, but virtually all of them will do it for a price. The fee ranges from $1500 to over $10,000—depending upon the risks, and the wealth of the client ordering the raid. There have been several suits instituted against detectives and against all of the participants involved in matrimonial raids charging assault and trespass. The costs of defending these suits and the risk to the detective of losing his license are such that these uninvited visits will not be undertaken without payment in full in advance. The risks, of course, are much greater when a raid is conducted outside of the marital home. It is one thing for a husband or a wife

° The use of evidence obtained in a marital raid has been narrowly upheld by New York's highest Court (*Sackler* v. *Sackler*, 15 N.Y. 2d 40) in a 4–3 decision, against the contention that the use of such evidence violated the Fourth Amendment of the United States Constitution which affords protection against unlawful searches and seizures.

to invite detectives, relatives, and friends to the house occupied by the parties and their children, there is much less legitimate right in inviting a raiding party to a hotel or to a separate apartment maintained by the husband or wife.

Although it is possible to be a smart "cheater," most detectives and matrimonial lawyers would agree that those who play around and don't get caught owe their success, not to their mates being clever, but simply to the fact that most of us do not have the desire, money, or perhaps just the courage to find out. Every detective maintains a portfolio of photographs to prove how the brightest and most imaginative of us get caught when suspecting mates really concentrate on checking up.

It is simply not in the spirit of marital infidelity to continually check to see if one is being followed; to take cabs, buses, and subways to trysting places; to never be seen in a private club or restaurant; to never go dancing; to use only pay phones; to never order for two when using a hotel's room service, etc. Even those who are the most cautious cheaters tend in time, through complacency or out of a spirit of adventure, to form patterns.

Darryl Klay, one of New York's prominent detectives, summed up why so few adulterers get away with their infidelity once the private detective is on their trail:

Sooner or later every adulterer or adulteress becomes arrogant and overconfident of his ability to outsmart the detective. The cheating husband or wife sooner or later gives a great deal of thought to what he or she is doing, and all cheaters arrive at a pattern that they think is invulnerable. It is only a matter of time when you beat them to death. Because they have established a pattern and pattern is death to the adulterer, it is our steppingstone to success.

I don't care what the pattern is, even if we have to get it piecemeal. Suppose we get two blocks today; suppose we get an address and a subway stop tomorrow. Finally we learn the neighborhood in which the parties are meeting; maybe the next day we narrow it down to two or three blocks. Maybe the next day or two we lose the couple we are trailing altogether, but if the pattern continues, just like a code, we will break it.

The only cheaters we have no luck with are the completely promiscuous ones. Those with a different guy or different girl every time they cheat are almost impossible to catch. The reason is simple; they don't establish a pattern.

Perhaps legislators should delve more deeply into the dynamics of marital affairs. We think they would be surprised to discover how many spouses simply do not want to know whether or not their mates are cheating. They would learn how many husbands and wives didn't really blame their mates even after they have been discovered. They would learn how many marriages continued even after a successful raid. They would at least take note of the fact that every act of marital infidelity is different from every other. They would perhaps become convinced that the institution of marriage can be preserved, as it has been for centuries, without legislative intervention designed to reward or punish. Married couples inclined to private sex habits cannot be controlled by legislative fiat.

The threat of economic sanctions does not deter infidelity any more than the threat of capital punishment deters the commission of murder. And while infidelity only rarely saves marriages, neither does it, standing alone, destroy them. And because each such act is committed in such a complicated and unique setting, its effect in arriving at a fair and equitable divorce settlement should not be preordained by statute, but should depend upon each different set of facts.

CHAPTER 14

Divorce Folklore and Miscellany

Herewith some miscellaneous reflections upon the divorce process which do not properly fit within the earlier chapters, and yet may be enlightening. They consist of clearly "unscientific" observations based solely on the experience of the lawyer-author of this book.

(a) *Fall and Winter Divorces.* Although statistics abound concerning how many divorces are granted in different states in the United States and even how many are granted on a month-to-month basis, none focus on when, in point of time, marital discord is likely to begin.

Yet there is a notable increase in lawyer consultations directly after the summer and directly after the Christmas-New Year holidays. And though there is no clear-cut distinction between the sorts of complaints a matrimonial lawyer hears in September and those he hears in January, there is a noticeably different texture and quality about them which is interesting and useful to observe.

In September, more than at other times, lawyers are met by angrier and more outraged spouses whose problems very often concern the moral transgressions of husbands and wives during the course of the summer:

HUSBAND: That ungrateful bitch, while I spent the summer working my head off in the hot city, she was screwing around with the lifeguard.

178

Or

HUSBAND: While I spent the summer in the city taking care of her God-damn cats, she spent the summer in a rented house at the beach, which I couldn't afford, giving parties for people I didn't know, ignoring the kids, and now she wants to buy the God-damn house. I just can't take her extravagances any more.

Or

WIFE: That son-of-a-bitch, while he has me stashed away at the beach, which he knows I hate, with three kids, a dog, two cats, and a canary, he has been screwing around in the city all week.

Or

WIFE: The man is just a cheap son-of-a-bitch. Everyone of our friends went away for the summer while Mr. Big Shot took the family away for one whole weekend. On top of that, he won't even air-condition the kids' room and one of them has a postnasal drip.

The fall complaints are angry, vituperative, bitter, and more unforgiving.

On the other hand, the sounds of marital discord in January strike a very different note. January is a time of depression, of sad reflection upon the end of another unhappy year. Christmas has come and gone and Santa Claus goofed again. The complaints are less accusatorial and less shrill, but more anguished:

EITHER: We are just not happy. We never go anywhere; life together for us is a nightmare.

Or

EITHER: I am forty (or fifty or sixty), and I just don't want to wait any longer. I have to change my life.

If there is validity to the foregoing observations, perhaps more lawyers, marriage counselors, doctors, psychologists, and couples themselves should consider the correlation, if any, between the season when marital combatants initiate the divorce process and the events which preceded it. How many marriages may have come apart simply because of the disproportionately tense aftermaths of a particularly irritating summer or a particularly depressing winter?

(b) *Summer Vacations.* A good deal more thought, in fact, should be given by married partners to the wisdom of separate summer vacations, with the husband remaining in the city while the wife and children spend all or part of the summer in the country.

To many couples this separation can offer a useful respite, a chance to exist independently with less pressure and with mutual opportunities for isolated and often healthy reflection.

But it is even more obvious that any prolonged separation between husband and wife creates the risk that one or both will "become involved" in some sexual meanderings, however slight. Summertime flings have provided some couples with the sexual release that one or both partners needed, and indeed, many husbands and wives look forward eagerly to the summer for just this reason.

But the hard fact is that the summer vacations which turn out to last forever are legion; as are the temptations they invite.

(c) *The Lure of the Singles.* Buddy Hackett, the comedian, said that he got married because he was the last member of his gang to hold out. He then said that he was a fool for not realizing that he could have joined another gang. The reverse is true. Many people divorce because all of their friends have parted. It is a natural trait of the newly divorced to convince others (by way of convincing themselves) of the glories and the freedom of divorce. You will never learn what the score really is by talking to your recently divorced friends; and people should seriously consider joining another gang if their discontentment stems from envy of their single friends.

(d) *Beware of the Lover Who Sees You through It.* It is a familiar phenomenon that spouses with paramours invite their lawyer to meet the prospective "lucky" man or woman. While this is more often done by the woman in the guise of "I would like you to explain this to Harry because he is very interested in marrying me," it is also done by husbands with prospective new mates, most often out of a sense of pride. Beware, dear friends, of the lover who sees you through it. He or she often disappears almost as soon as the wax on the decree hardens. This generalization has, of course, been proven wrong on many occasions. But the countless lovers who make it worth noting looked just as sincere to client and lawyer as the ones who have not borne the generalization out.

Perhaps one of the reasons why so many lovers "cop out" is that they see their married intendeds under circumstances not usually conducive to courtship. Long association with a lover engaged in marital travail exposes some unfamiliar and unpalatable views—his penury, her overreaching, their emotional outbursts and vindictiveness, the airing of ugly rumors (and the fragile defenses to such rumors)—all of which have a dampening effect on romance.

(e) *The Ransom of Red Chief Theory*. It will be recalled that in O. Henry's famous short story the kidnapers of a child rued their venal act when the parents refused to accede to lesser and lesser demands by the kidnapers. The parents simply didn't want the little brat! Very often, mothers with custody are plagued by recalcitrant husbands who fail to make support payments, who continuously fail to observe their visitation privileges, and who generally disregard all of their postmarital obligations. Jack Friedlander, a well-known Washington, D.C., lawyer, frequently advises his divorcée-clients under such circumstances simply to drop the children off at the husband's office one day. He claims that this ploy has had a remarkably beneficial effect. Although it is fraught with danger, it may well work where the wife knows her mate.

(f) *Marital "Stool Pigeon"—the Backfire*. In many bitter divorce proceedings, one combatant threatens the other with the exposure to various public authorities of information confided during the marriage. Wives threaten husbands that they will go to the Internal Revenue Service, report large accumulations of cash, disclose the existence of a Swiss bank account, etc. Husbands, for obvious reasons, make such threats far less often.

Worse, those threats are frequently acted upon—usually with tragic consequences to the squealer. In the first place, the Internal Revenue Service is deluged with "information" from wives. The "information" is very often useless to the government because it is skimpy, because the wife can't testify against her husband, and because by the time the government gets around to investigating it, the parties have either reconciled or have come to a mutual agreement and the wife readily admits that she was mistaken.

And it should be, but is not, obvious that where the wife has sufficient information to get the husband in trouble, she is only serving to diminish the proceeds out of which her settlement is ultimately to come. Needless to say, courts invariably take a very dim view of turncoat wives or husbands.

In one case an enormously wealthy wife, with millions of dollars of assets in the United States, reported to the government the existence of a foreign bank account of her husband's. The wife's lawyer in an outrageous burst of enthusiasm proceeded to claim that at least half of the foreign account, if not all, belonged to her. The net effect of this act was to subject the wife to astronomical claims by the government for back taxes, interest penalties, and possible criminal liability. Whatever assets the husband had were out of the country; and because of this action by the wife's counsel, an agreement was prepared far more favorable to the husband than he could have ever achieved had his mate not sung her unfortunate song.

(g) *Substituting Lawyers.* It is perfectly obvious that sometimes lawyers and clients do not "hit it off." It is then necessary, for a variety of reasons on the client's or the lawyer's part, that new counsel be engaged. There is an unfortunate tendency, however, on the part of new lawyers, as well as clients with new advocates, to escalate whatever terms have previously been offered, regardless of how sound, generous, and fair they were.

It is true, however, that where new counsel is engaged after marital negotiations have taken place, the other side, disheartened, becomes resigned to the probability that whatever offer has been on the table must be improved, or a trial endured.

Neither clients nor subsequent counsel should delude themselves, though, that the offer is going to get any better. Lawyers who have heard only their clients' side of the story very often find, when they are substituted for prior counsel, that the offer that had previously been made was perfectly adequate and should have been accepted. The new lawyer should not hesitate to make that fact known to his client, and the client should not hesitate to accept such advice—and pay for it.

(h) *"Ill Move out of the State."* Wives are constantly threatened by husbands who claim that since they are losing their home and children, they will give up their jobs, move to another state or to a foreign country, etc., etc. While there are no statistics on what percentage of such threats are ever acted upon, and while it is most unlikely that a husband will really skip town to avoid supporting his family, it can happen. Where the husband has no "other woman," or where he has friends and relatives in another state and no business which requires his attention, the threat is real. It is, of course, possible to follow the husband and sue him for support wherever he goes. There are proceedings available in almost every state by which neglected wives and children may seek support through legal machinery in their own state, even though the husband is in another one. However, where the husband does actually leave the state, and where the wife lacks sufficient funds, interstate husband-chasing is time-consuming and expensive.

Sometimes husbands are actually chased out of their states; forced, in desperation, to avoid agreements or decrees which are so harsh that they cannot be complied with because the wife, through bitterness or vindictiveness, will not voluntarily offer any relief. On the contrary, she very often relentlessly seeks compliance with agreements and decrees, knowing the husband can't live up to them. Sometimes husbands will sign or agree to anything to get rid of their wives, or to free themselves to marry new lovers. They then find themselves trapped, and when all else fails, seek escape elsewhere.

(i) *Clients as Do-It-Yourself Lawyers and Investigators.*

HUSBAND: I am a better lawyer than you are. You couldn't get my wife out of the house by going to court. Well she is out.
HUSBAND'S LAWYER: She left?
HUSBAND: Bag and baggage and she is not about to come back.
HUSBAND'S LAWYER: What happened?
HUSBAND: My wife can't stand dogs, so I rented two Doberman pinschers. They growled at her like she was the meat in the Alpo ad.
LAWYER'S SECRETARY (*entering the room*): I thought you would like to see these papers that were just delivered.
HUSBAND'S LAWYER (*after glancing at the papers*): This is what is known as an "order of show cause" which directs us to appear before the court tomorrow to explain why an order should not be made either kicking you and the dogs out of the house or directing you to pay for your wife's hotel bills. By the way, she is staying at the Waldorf-Astoria.

Another Scene

WIFE: I don't need a detective. I have a wonderful family that is getting me all the dope on my husband. My brother Harry is friendly with my husband's boss. My niece Terry lives across the street from my husband, and tells me every time he sneezes. My nephew Herbert works in the same building in which my husband has his office and he has been checking my husband's mail every morning because he gets to work before my husband or anyone in his office. Not only that, but my husband has been dating my cousin Marilyn's girl friend . . .
LAWYER'S SECRETARY (*entering the room*): I thought you would like to see these papers right away.
LAWYER (*after glancing at the papers*): This bundle of papers requires you to explain in court why a protective order should not be issued enjoining you, Harry, Terry, Herbert, and Marilyn from invading your husband's privacy. . . .

While marital investigation can be very helpful, it must be done under the supervision of a lawyer. What is acceptable snooping by investigators is condemned very strongly by courts when done with a heavy hand by clients, their friends, and family.

(j) *You Married Him, Your Lawyer Didn't.*

WIFE: That son-of-a-bitch won't turn the TV on [or off], and he keeps smoking cigars because he knows I hate them.

Or

WIFE: He is out until four a.m. every morning and he deliberately wakes me up when he comes home.

Or

WIFE: He refuses to visit the children, and when he brings them home on the few occasions when he does see the kids, they have stomach-aches from too much pizza and ice cream.

Or

HUSBAND: She is driving me crazy. She is on the phone all night long and I can't sleep.

Or

HUSBAND: Every time I pick my son up she has him dressed up like Little Lord Fauntleroy just because she knows it bugs me.

Or

HUSBAND: She is never home and she keeps leaving the children with the French governess, who can hardly speak a word of English.

Lawyers are powerless to redress all the annoying petty grievances which exist during the divorce process and judges simply will not intervene in every family squabble. You married your mate, your lawyer didn't. And if he or she is a pain in the neck, it is a price you must pay while getting out. While lawyers and judges can strive to undo a bad marriage and to see to it that wives and children receive a fair amount of support, the judicial process is not geared to changing personalities. The law does not change obnoxious oafs into pussycats or shrill hysterics into doves.

A great deal can be done about truly disruptive and violent behavior patterns that realistically and materially threaten a spouse's health. Courts will quickly squelch such behavior, particularly if there are children being subjected to it. But it is then and only then that the lawyers and courts can accomplish anything that is meaningful.

Judges will not decide whether children should wear galoshes, whether husbands should or should not smoke cigars, whether wives should refrain from using the telephone too much, or whether or not Aunt Tillie is a bad influence on Junior.

(k) *Profile of the Perfect Client.* Somewhat tongue in cheek, we offer the attributes of the kind of clients, wife and husband, which a lawyer would like to represent.

WIFE:

A. Plain to pretty (judges and juries assume that "beautiful people" will do all right by themselves).
B. Mild-mannered, soft-spoken—cursing is out, crying moderately is in.
C. Unable to earn money.
D. Able to create and be industrious, e.g., accomplished cook, painter, sculptress, member of voluntary organizations.
E. Faithful.
F. Good mother.
G. First marriage unless prior mate died, or, better yet, went crazy.
H. Physical disability (mental disability is out—it's considered malingering if mild, or the wife can't be trusted with funds if it's worse).

HUSBAND:

A. Business on decline—s-l-o-w-l-y—("instant failure" is easily detected).
B. Good father.
C. Employed (tax returns are reliable).
D. Neat and plain dresser—button-downs are in, jewelry and moccasins are out.
E. Supports another family or aging relatives.

F. One other woman is starting to be "in"—woman-chasing is out.

G. Must come to court by subway or train and never in a company-owned car.

(1) *The Arithmetic of Divorce.* Nobody should visit a lawyer seeking a divorce or separation without having done his homework. The basic material with which a lawyer works are three sets of figures: (a) the personal and real property that is owned by the parties and the children individually and jointly. A realistic assessment of the value of the house, the car, the furniture, and all other real estate and personal property should be prepared. How much is in stocks, bonds, checking accounts, and savings accounts? Against those assets, what debts exist? How much is owed for household bills; how much is owed to the bank and others for loans? What insurance policies exist and in the case of life insurance policies, do they have a cash surrender value? (b) What is the income earning record of both spouses over the last five years? Where are the income-tax returns? If you have them, bring them to your lawyer. (c) What records reflect how the parties have been living over the past several years? While income-tax records are useful, particularly in the case of parties employed by others, they are not determinative where the parties maintain a standard of living greatly in excess of what the income-tax returns reflect.

As we have seen, courts have awarded as support for the wife and children, more money than a husband reports as his entire income. But it will not do so without substantial proof of hidden income. You should list exactly how much money is expended in the course of a year for the benefit of the family. How much for rent; how much for clothing; how much for the tailor, the cleaner, the hairdresser, the barber; how much for cigarettes, for carfare, for the children's allowance, for vacations; how much for insurance premiums, for poodle-clipping, for the maid, for the gardener, for the chauffeur, etc. *All* expenses regardless of their size should be listed. If bank statements and canceled checks are available, they should be brought to the lawyer's office.

There is a great deal of resistance to preparing these records by clients. One of the reasons is that more often than not clients become depressed when they have to face the fact that they cannot account for sufficient income to provide for all of the expenses, and they become doubly depressed when they realize that the husband in order to establish a new home will have to incur many new expenses out of the same amount of money. Depressing or not, the figures must be prepared and you will not learn very much from your lawyer unless he has these figures at his disposal.

CHAPTER 15

Aftermath

I. *Living Alone*

So now you are free. Finally—after weeks and months and millennia—the decree is there.

You are a man and not a husband. You are a woman and not a wife. You share many of the same feelings, and many that are different.

What you probably most share in common is relief. At last it's over: the agony, the bickering, the delays, the recriminations, the despair, the endless legalities, the lawyers. Loser or winner —in the sense of money or possessions or pride or hope or children (all shuffled on the checkerboard of divorce)—the bitter game is over.

But it isn't over. It's only just begun.

What has begun is a wholly different life, not only within yourself but outside of yourself. What do you do with this life, now that—presumably—it is your own?

There are no typical divorced people. But there are typical situations faced by them the moment they are divorced. And although their reactions have something in common, how men and women handle their new condition still varies considerably.

Usually, she has the children. The older ones hardly need to be told that "Daddy and I haven't been getting along very well

189

together, so we . . ." (By older, we mean practically any child over six.) Educated (if that is the word) by the street, by television, and in school corridors, they are precocious beyond anything dreamed of (or born) thirty years ago. They may miss the presence of the father but they are told Daddy will visit them and take them out, and anyway he wasn't around that much before. Divorce and sex are household words.

As for the teen-agers, many of them are already pretty contemptuous of the adult hang-ups about marriage, morality and social, legal, and religious sanctions. They consider love to be above and beyond legalities, and although they will probably marry, they are convinced—as are all new generations—that they can make a better and freer job of it than their parents.

Still, it is the mother who usually gets the custody of the children; and the pleasures and burdens of having to care for them give her a sense of continuity and usefulness that can soften the transition and mute the pain.

Whether she herself feels lost—or released—by her husband's absence, other factors crowd in on her because of it. She is suddenly swamped by the technicalities of living, foremost of which is the management of money. Suddenly, she not only has to take care of people and food and clothing, but of financial records and transactions and expenditures that her husband had usually managed before.

This is the direct result, as we have emphasized several times, of a fatal lack of candor and communication between husband and wife on the mutual concern of money: who has what, who spends what, who saves what, who invests what.

A very large measure of the difficulties, unpleasantness, and delays of divorce proceedings lie precisely in this lack of candor and planning both before and during the now-dissolved marriage. Those who doubt that this omission is a major cause of divorce, might consider a private poll recently made by a professor of obstetrics at the University of California, Dr. George M. Melody.

Topping his list of roots of marital discord is financial problems, 25 per cent; adultery, 15 per cent; personal incompatibility, 10 per cent; and last, sexual problems, 3 per cent.

There are, of course, households in which the wife handled the money, either because she had it or because her husband—possibly a creative man with no talent for money and less desire for dealing with it—left such matters to her.

But the average wife is now embroiled with, and tormented by, matters which her husband has been trained to handle since his first job. The self-reliant husband may be left poorer by divorce, but no less capable of handling the economic realities than before.

Children and money, in fact, are the only two binding agents that force the newly divorced husband and wife to see each other, for varying periods of time after the decree.

These confrontations are perhaps the most delicate, difficult, and painful of all human contacts. When a man and woman have lived with each other for twenty or ten or even five years, the connective tissues of this intimacy die hard. The habits of affection and companionship—if they did indeed exist—linger on. And a tone of voice, a turn of the head, a certain laugh can twist a knife in either rejector or rejected.

If the bitterness goes deep, the chill can be anesthetic. But very often the mere fact that a man and woman are no longer required to live with and love each other allows them to view each other with different eyes; even as friends.

For most, perhaps, this new vision is long in coming or never comes at all. But for many, it is the optimum solution, certainly for their children, but also for their own interior peace.

Hate we repeat, is corrosive, eating away at a productive life, blighting the instinct and capacity for love which alone can free the human soul. The woman who keeps calling her ex-husband an S.O.B. for the rest of her life, the husband who keeps telling his new wife or lover what a horror his former wife was, may have "right" on their side (they won their case, didn't they?), but betray their small substance as human beings.

If blame they must, then blame themselves for having made

poor choices in the partners they first vowed to cherish. Or blame the illusions which cloud too many of our judgments.

The inexcusable blame is the one transmitted to the children of divorce, usually by their mother, since she is probably their custodian. The woman who presents an image of their father as a monster or a weakling or a bum does them as well as herself irreparable harm. She need not make him a hero, but if affection still exists between children and father, the constant conflict between what he is and what he is presented as being either ruins their relationship or turns the child violently against the mother.

Where, on the other hand, former husband and former wife can treat each other casually and lightly as friends who once had much in common but now lead new lives, often with different partners, the young may not only feel at ease but even benefit from the widening family circle. Of course, relationships with a new stepfather or stepmother may be delicate or even unhappy. The young may deeply resent, at least at first, any presumed substitute for their real parent as a strange invader of their lives. But time, patience, and compassion usually manage to overcome this resistance—especially when the new partners of either parent present themselves as friends rather than surrogates. The addition of new backgrounds and homes, of new half-sisters or half-brothers, is more pleasing than not to gregarious youth since it provides alternatives to the "nuclear" family and outlets for greater activity.

But only friendship between divorced partners can bring this about. And friendship can happen; it is happening more and more as moral stigmas fade and increased diversity in the ways people choose to live breaks down old barriers.

II. *The Different Lives*

Next to hate, which can turn inward as well as outward, bitterness and self-pity are the two most damaging human emotions. They eat into the vitals, they block the creative juices of life, they dry up the springs of love.

Both self-pity and bitterness are, also, the most common fall-outs from the fission of divorce, and, particularly in women, self-poisoning.

Why women, particularly? One might assume two major causes. One, that the majority of them are far more dependent on the props of marriage than men, having lived on, for, and through men for many years. Two, that finding new mates in the middle years is far more difficult for women than for men. The market for "mature" divorcées is, in a youth culture as obsessive as ours, very narrow.

When lovers for either are waiting in the wings for the final decree, the situation is markedly altered. The dreams of a new life leave little place for bitterness even when they may be tinged with guilt toward the rejected and once-loved partner.

But even if it is the man, and not the woman, who has been divorced by his mate because of a rival in love, bitterness has little time to take over. He has his work, his profession, or his business. As the extra man, he is highly desirable socially. He can, far more freely than women, even now, drink out and talk out his marital woes at some friendly bar. (A female doing this is usually viewed as a mess or a menace—to be avoided. Unfortunately, she often is.)

What a man misses most are his children and what comforts of home his wife provided, particularly if she was a good cook and housekeeper. After enjoying them—if not always his mate —for years, it is irksome to have to worry about laundry and cleaners and food; and a motel room or a furnished apartment offers few pleasures or solaces except the freedom to import sexual diversion when needed and enjoy television and newspapers without the running comment of a loquacious wife.

But the truly domestic man—and there are many—acutely misses, for at least a time, the sounds and smell of home and kitchen, the clatter of children, and the softness of the accustomed chair by the TV set or before the fire. Rights of visitation with his offspring seldom compensate for their sudden comings and goings and sayings and proximity, even when they are intermittently a nuisance.

As for the natural twinges of anger or jealousy he may feel when he thinks of his wife with another man, his daily absorptions in the world of work allows him to turn them off more and more as time goes on and his friends provide him with social diversions that blur past images and with companions capable of providing future ones.

As we indicated earlier, men have a much greater capacity for turning off purely personal concerns, simply by avoiding self-confrontation, than women. They cannot shut them off entirely, but the fragility of their egos has built up a defense mechanism against facts or feelings of rejection that would diminish their potency as males. They cannot afford the indulgence of self-pity precisely because it *is* self-diminishing.

One state of mind, however, is shared by men and women as they contemplate their postdivorce lives. It is the illusion of freedom battling with the sense of failure. Again, the sense of failure is more acute in women because they have for long been conditioned to believe that their prime index of success is measured by pleasing a man. If their husbands no longer wish to be married to them, their first instinct (as in sexual "failure") is to believe that something is wrong with *them:* something they lack as women. It is, conversely, difficult for many men to believe themselves inadequate.

But the illusion of freedom ultimately prevails for both. New life, a new partner, with no repetition of the mistakes and misconceptions on which their previous marriage had foundered. "Out there is someone who understands me, who knows what I really am, and what I could really be."

Often the dream materializes. Many second marriages not only seem but are considerably happier than the first because both partners have learned the hard way what to bring to each other instead of what to take from each other.

Statistics make this abundantly clear. Although divorces are up, especially among the young (and up 28 per cent among marriages that have lasted twenty to twenty-four years), the 1960s record three hundred thousand more marriages a year than in the previous decade, and half of these were remarriages. In other words, one out of six of the men and women newly united had been married before. Dr. Paul Glick, the Chief of the Population Division of the Census Bureau, says that: "Those who remarry are much more likely to remain in their second marriage than persons married only once are to remain in their first."

Clearly, a number of second marriages become, in time, repetitions of the first. Not only do many men automatically gravitate to the same kind of woman they married before (known evils are better than unknown?), but the capacity for fundamental change in human beings diminishes with the years.

Instead of freedom and growth, the patterns of familiarity and dependence form again; habit prevails and the sense of renewal gradually wanes.

Yet what of the "freedom" of the divorced partner whose prospects for remarriage are either dim or nonexistent?

After the mutual battering and upheaval of divorce itself—finally achieved, at what final cost to the man or woman involved—the comparative calm that follows the settlement is, to say the least, illusory. It is a kind of decompression that produces a variety of side effects, not all desirable.

For the one who has a new partner waiting at the open gates, the sense of freedom and renewal may seem euphoric. For the one who has no one waiting, it may loom as a frightening void. In either case—and whatever was said to the other and about the other during the long litigation and legal wrangles—guilt dogs the footsteps of the first, and rejection encloses the second in a black cloud.

Both may have planned what their lives would be like after the final decree: whether she would stay in the house or apartment, or move to a smaller one, or take a job; whether he would move into his lover's apartment until they found another.

But these decisions, externally important as they might seem, are much less so than the emotional attitudes impelling either to action or passivity, to relief and joy, to release, or to a loneliness even worse than the dead marriage.

Let's take a not-so-imaginary couple. Ned and Mary had thought for fifteen years that they had a good marriage. That it had lost its excitement during the last five years, that they slept together less than once a week (usually after Ned had had three or more drinks), each had tacitly accepted as inevitable.

Until, of course, one of those "kind friends" told Mary that Ned's pleasures and interests lay elsewhere.

The weeks that followed were such agony for both that even before divorce proceedings were under way, Ned performed the classic act of moving to his club, leaving several of his suits in the closet to haunt Mary, and no sound of the key turning in the front door at 6 p.m. to torture her every evening. The empty bed next to her is bad enough, but the late afternoon is worse. It is the loudest silence she has ever heard.

If no one telephones, she flips through her address book, calls some of her best friends, single or married, and says "What are you doing tonight?" or tomorrow, or Saturday. If she is with a group, she drinks a lot and very fast and tries to be brave and noble and even funny, fooling no one. If she is with a woman friend (single men, unless they love her as a human being, flee from the mangled divorcée), the floodgates open. It helps Mary temporarily, but the next time the friend is very busy.

If Mary is more sensible than many women, she will begin immediately to involve herself in something outside herself, politics or social service, or use whatever talent she once had and never developed. She may join classes for adults at the nearest university or take postgraduate courses in whatever subject most engrossed her in her college years.

If she has "let herself go"—the usual concomitant, rather than cause, of not being desired—she plans to do something about it. Mary is basically an attractive woman, with style and grace. But when a husband stops looking at his wife, or saying that he likes her better in blue than red, the tendency among most women is resignation rather than renewed efforts to please or excite. The reinforcement of sexual attraction is a two-way street, and if a husband reduces this support not only to token infrequent love-making, but to avoidance of mere physical contact, his wife's belief in herself as a woman is bound to wither. This then leads to the fatal words which men rightly abhor: "You don't love me any more!" or "You don't care what I put on, you don't even look." (Or touch, or pat, or ruffle the hair, or whack the fanny.) The psychic hurt then becomes the physical slump. Mary feels middle-aged and looks it.

But again, if she knows this, she will do something about it. She will exercise, she will change her hair-do, alter her style and—if she can afford it—have facials or massage. These superficial ploys can't erase the ache, but they can bring back the nerve. And with nerve, the bounce returns, a way of walking and looking that men recognize and respond to: here is a woman.

We are not talking of new love. This is rare, and flees when consciously sought. It merely means that Mary is not an amputated but a whole human being. She cannot stop thinking of Ned and hating the woman he loves (until that too, in time, is muted), but now, after months of taking—from loyal friends, from the hospitality of slight acquaintances—she is able to give in her own right. She is not living on pity or charity (the "extra woman" is so considered by social women planning their table-seating) but on what charm and gaiety she can bring to others. In so doing she has rediscovered, after long if contented submergence to Ned Jones, a woman called Mary Smith: herself.

This is the hopeful, if hardly universal pattern; the result of conscious planning and instinctive vitality. The unhappy divorcées are those who lack the latter and are too drowned in the past to care for the future, women who are natural victims, living off their suffering as animals live off their fat. They spend their lives doing little things that repeat former little patterns, suffer from a succession of little ailments, complain because they see so little of their friends, have so little money, envy so many women. They comfort themselves with bridge, antiques, and local gossip, wondering why they are bored, worrying about their house, their possessions, their personal safety, and young people protesting.

A third category of women, once divorced, have a very definite plan: to latch on to the first presentable man they can find, not only because they are starved for sex or love, but to get back at their former husbands. Right after the decree, they wear dresses slit down to the nipples and up to the thighs, scrambled gypsy hair (or wigs), heavy eye make-up and super-gloss lipstick in a new "vibrant" color. Their ex-husbands might not recognize them.

Other men do: but hardly as wives. In any case, Carol (we might call her) has a ball, balling. The exhilaration of thrashing around with a different man every week or two, and sometimes twice a week, does wonders for her ego even though not all of them really get *to* her. Some have nothing to say either before, during, or after intercourse, others are instant lovers: no preamble, thanks, see you, will call.

Carol is likely in the end to settle for a very dull man, recently divorced, who bears a marked resemblance to her former husband including the latter's indifference—ultimately to be revealed—to whatever she's wearing, so long as it's not provocative.

But what of the rejected man, divorced by his wife? If we have seemed so far to stress the problems of the rejected woman, it is largely because of two factors: her social and economic dependence, which has made her less self-reliant, less able to cope with the manifold decisions now crowding in on her; and again, the mournful prospect that her chances for remarriage, unlike those of men, dwindle progressively after forty.

But these differences in no way minimize the emotional shock felt by a husband rejected by his wife, and the sense of loss and inadequacy are intensified by the bleakness of single existence.

Men, too, have acquired long habits of dependence. They may

manage their businesses or their professions competently or expertly, but the majority of husbands have never had to learn how to feed themselves, create a comfortable or attractive environment, or cope directly with laundries, cleaners, domestic appliances, and the endless details of daily living assumed by women.

The more imaginative may discover in time that they can cook better than their wives, or that they have innate talents for decoration never before allowed to be exercised. The young find nothing strange in these domestic creative expressions in a man, and society is very slowly beginning to view them not necessarily as aberrations but even—quaintly—as assets.

Yet the men without them—still the majority—find even minimal housekeeping for themselves not only tedious but confusing, and prefer to resign themselves to hotels, furnished rooms, or sublets and eat out rather than bother, except vestigially, with the "comforts of home."

So, often, this soundless aridity can force them into self-doubt and painful memory, and inevitably Out, to forget.

For most, of course, the job takes care of the day. But the nights must somehow be filled, the mind distracted, the flesh appeased. And for many, then, the dating game begins.

Friends are only too eager to introduce them to swingers or to a sympathetic divorcée, and married women friends start to look at them with a new and curious, if not always approving, eye.

So they take women out, or home, or both, and sometimes it's fun and sometimes it's ashes, and very often they cannot stop thinking of or comparing with or wanting the wife who didn't want them.

And if sex doesn't work, they wonder what's wrong with them; and if it does, they wonder why this particular woman is in their bed and they wish she'd go home because they have nothing to talk about.

And they wonder what their kids are doing, and how Alice is coping, and torture themselves with images of her in bed with Jack.

In time, of course, this too passes. Some day they will find the ideal girl or woman, or think they have. Some day she will make them a new home and bear them new children, and the past is allowed to recede without bitterness.

But man is at heart a romantic: more so, we believe, than women, who might deny this. Women too have "ideal" dreams and images of what love or life should be, and one of the most pernicious and tenacious of these, fostered in them from childhood, is the wedding, the ring, the cake, and love ever after. Pernicious because it is contrived, promoted, and packaged as a life-guarantee of "happiness" and security.

Men know better than this. Outwardly they go through the accepted paces but inwardly they recognize the myth.

They want more from a woman than security or companionship. They want a vision: to love, to defend, even to worship.

And when the vision disintegrates—when slowly and then sharply through rejection and divorce they begin to see that they have been used and are now of no use to the one they loved—the hurt goes deep.

III. *To Whom It Does Not Concern*

Divorce is a private and not a community matter. Society plays—should play—no part in the dissolution of a marriage, even if it is an audience gossiping on the sidelines.

We are not talking of divorce between celebrities: whatever they do becomes automatically public property. But even surrounding friends of two nonpublic people in the throes of divorce should not join the act, simply because it concerns only the man and wife who are dissolving their marriage.

They may act as comforters and supporters, but never as co-litigants or judges. When they do, they engage in a process known as "taking sides." However gratifying this may be to the person whose side they espouse, they are doing them no good. They are merely enforcing attitudes—the animosity and self-pity described here before—which ultimately do harm to the cause and life of their champion.

Yet divorced wives—more than their male ex-partners—reach for this allegiance as a lifesaver. They not only crave this loyalty of friends, they solicit it. And there is nothing sweeter to their ears than hearing their friends tell them what a total slob or brute Larry was to leave this lovely, adorable, attractive wife for some call-girl, model, or other, or that rich bitch.

Even worse, when they hear that one of their so-called friends is actually *seeing* Larry, and even having him to *dinner,* that traitor is now the enemy. It never occurs to this kind of woman that some of their friends might have liked both of them, together and individually, as human beings, and that the fact they have parted—however unhappily—in no way alters affection for either.

If men are less prone to muster this battle line-up on their side, and against their ex-wives, it is again that they are much more averse to public emotion than women. They may spill over in bars, preferably to strangers, yet, if only because it is a reflection on their choice of a mate, they do not relish their ex-wife being called a bitch by others, even if they concur.

No one, on the other hand, who has not endured the pain of divorce can know the immense sustaining help provided by friends who offer not only shoulders to cry on, or ears to listen, but the reassurance that they wholly accept and value you at a time when the person you married has ostensibly stopped doing either.

For that matter, if divorce was inevitable, society as a whole accepts it with far more ease now than it did even a decade ago. Ideal as the vision of an enduring and loving union still is, the fragmentation of our lives in every area, global to communal to individual, affects even those who most deplore it. So does the exploding emphasis on freedom, for the many as well as the few, as a human right.

The only holdouts against divorce are the very devout or the very remote—geographically and chronologically—from present realities.

So the fall-out from the fission of divorce affects only the divorced (and their children), and any attempt on the part of either to divide others because of their own division is not only foolish but self-defeating.

The concept of who was right and who was wrong has no place in the infinite complexity of a married relationship or the social judgments that follow its dissolution.

Nor of who failed whom.

Index